0-76

Columbia University

Contributions to Education

Teachers College Series

No. 389

AMS PRESS
NEW YORK

DAY SCHOOLS VS. INSTITUTIONS FOR THE DEAF

A DETAILED ANALYSIS OF CERTAIN VARIATIONS IN THE
ABILITIES, ENVIRONMENT, AND HABITS OF DEAF
PUPILS, WITH AN EVALUATION OF THEIR
EFFECT ON EDUCATIONAL ACHIEVEMENT

BY

C. C. UPSHALL, Ph.D.

BUREAU OF PUBLICATIONS
Teachers College, Columbia University
NEW YORK CITY
1929

Library of Congress Cataloging in Publication Data

Upshall, Charles Cecil, 1901–
   Day schools vs. institutions for the deaf.

   Reprint of the 1929 ed., issued in series: Teachers
College, Columbia University. Contributions to edu-
cation, no. 389.
   Originally presented as the author's thesis, Columbia.
   Bibliography: p.
   1. Deaf—Education—United States. I. Title.
II. Series: Columbia University. Teachers College.
Contributions to education, no. 389.
HV2530.U7 1972   371.9'122   71-177686
ISBN 0-404-55389-3

Reprinted by Special Arrangement with Teachers
College Press, New York, New York

From the edition of 1929, New York
First AMS edition published in 1972
Manufactured in the United States

AMS PRESS, INC.
NEW YORK, N. Y.   10003

ACKNOWLEDGMENTS

The author is deeply indebted to Dr. Rudolf Pintner for his constant encouragement and many helpful suggestions. Through his instrumentality the National Research Council made available the records upon which the study is based. The author wishes to express his deep appreciation of the courtesy of this organization. He is indebted especially to Mr. I. S. Fusfeld and Mr. H. E. Day under whose direction the data were collected during 1924 and 1925.*

Permission to use the Institute of Educational Research occupational rating scale was granted by the Institute through Mrs. Zaida Miner. The author takes this occasion to express his thanks. To Dr. H. D. Kitson and Dr. P. Symonds for many valuable criticisms, to Mr. C. Derryberry, Mrs. Zaida Miner, Miss S. M. Bouche, and Miss E. M. Davis for their helpful suggestions and to Miss Rosalind Blum for her generous assistance in the preparation of the manuscript the author is greatly indebted.

The most grateful acknowledgments are due those of the author's personal friends who soothed him many times in small but important ways during the long hours of calculations and tabulations that this study has entailed.

C. C. Upshall

* The reports made by the National Research Council on the data collected appear in the following volumes of the *American Annals of the Deaf:* LXX, 991-421 (1925); LXXI, 97-135, 284-348 (1926); LXII, 2-34, 377-414 (1927); LXIII, 1-36, 184-201, 273-309 (1928). The collected report, "A Survey of American Schools for the Deaf, 1924-25," was issued by the National Research Council at Washington during 1928.

CONTENTS

CHAPTER I

OUTLINE OF THE STUDY

This study is a comparison of deaf pupils twelve years of age or older in Day Schools and Institutions for the deaf in the United States. The analysis is based on measurements of the following variables: chronological age, intelligence, educational achievement, age of becoming deaf, age of starting to school, number of years in schools for normal hearing children, number of years in schools for deaf children, amount of residual hearing, occupation of father, nationality, and dominant language spoken in the home. The problems which this study attempts to solve are:

1. How real is the difference between the Day Schools and the Institutions in each of the variables studied?

2. Are the Day Schools accomplishing more, as measured by the Pintner Educational Survey Test than the Institutions, when the children in each are made as comparable as possible?

3. What relationships exist between each of the variables and educational achievement as measured by the Pintner Educational Survey Test?

4. What are the interrelationships which exist among the variables themselves?

The more important data and methods of this study are summarized in this chapter.

1. Children whose records were incomplete or inaccurate in regard to the variables concerned in this study (except language spoken at home and father's occupation) were excluded.

2. Only children from twelve years of age to seventeen inclusive have been included.

3. The children retained for study were found to be distributed over the United States almost exactly as all the children included in the National Research Council Investigation and approximately as the total deaf population is distributed.

4. The Institutional children were divided into two groups for preliminary study. One group comprised 311 cases matched with an equal number of Day School children for chronological age and mental ability as measured by the Pintner Non-Language Test; the other group comprised 1,159 cases.

In this study the following procedures were used:

1. The method of percentages with graphical presentation was used to establish the similarity of distribution between the total deaf population in the United States, the total group studied by the National Research Council, and the group selected for this investigation.

2. Matching was employed in order to make a group from the Institutions more nearly comparable with the Day School group in respect to the factors which influence educational achievement.

3. The differences between the two types of schools were evaluated by means of statistical formulæ for estimating the chances in a hundred that the true difference between the means would be above zero.

4. The coefficient of variation was used to study the similarities and differences between the Day Schools and the Institutions in regard to variability.

5. The correlation technique was used to find the relationships which exist between the variables in both the Day Schools and the Institutions.

6. The correlation ratio was computed for all variables with the Educational Survey Test score.

7. The Blakeman short test for linearity was applied in all cases where both the Pearson product-moment correlation coefficient and the correlation ratio were computed.

8. All correlations were plotted so that pronounced curvilinearity could be readily detected.

9. The bi-serial r technique was used in studying foreigners.

10. The contingency technique was used in studying occupations.

CHAPTER II

OUTLINE OF CONDITIONS WHICH LED TO THIS STUDY

The special disability of deaf people has interested educators for centuries. In the United States the education of this class of people has received attention for over a century. Shortly after John Stanford [1] * had tried to teach a few deaf children in New York City, a school for the deaf, the New York Institution, was estblished there. [22] A little later one was opened in Virginia. These, however, were not then made permanent. Through the work of Thomas Hopkins Gallaudet, the first permanent school for the deaf was opened on April 15, 1817, in Hartford, Connecticut. [2] This type of education has continued to expand to the present time.

Methods for instructing the deaf evolved slowly because the methods used for educating normal hearing children were manifestly not applicable without radical changes. In order to establish communication, substitutes for language were originated such as the "sign-methods," "the spelling method," "the speech method" and its supplement, lip reading.

These and other methods of imparting instruction which have been used in this country have gradually crystallized until three or four have gained precedence, e.g., the manual, the auricular, and the oral methods. For many years proponents of these methods gave lengthy reasons illustrated by hand-picked examples to show that the particular method they were sponsoring was the best; but neither the reasons nor the examples were forceful enough to carry conviction to the opposing side.

Soon after the beginning of the twentieth century, standardized tests for measuring mental ability and educational achievement began to be devised and used. During 1916 Pintner and Paterson published two articles describing their experiments concerning

* Bracketed numbers refer to sources listed on pages 103 and 104.

3

the learning ability of deaf children. [29, 30] They followed this preliminary work within a year or two with performance tests [31] which might be used to measure the mental ability of deaf children.

During the World War the group test was evolved as a result of the necessity of testing large numbers of men in the army within a very short time. [38] In 1919 Pintner published the non-language group test [26] of mental ability used in this study. His test of educational achievement [27] was published soon after to be used with the mental test for survey purposes. Thus, within a period of four years there was made available to those interested in the education of the deaf, standardized mental and educational tests which could be used to evaluate the ability and achievement of deaf children.

The norms [28] for both the Pintner Non-Language Test and the Pintner Educational Survey Test were based upon the performance of normal hearing children. Stimulated by Pintner and Paterson's work, Reamer [32] undertook an intensive study of deaf children by means of the instruments recently made available. Her study reveals the fact that the deaf are, in general, inferior to hearing children in both mental ability and educational achievement. They are retarded to a greater degree in the latter than in the former. Other conclusions will be referred to in the chapters which follow.

A committee of men [8] prominent in education of the deaf, met in July, 1919, and formulated certain definite problems connected with the education of the deaf, among which appeared the following: (a) methods and means of teaching; (b) progress of children in academic courses; (c) progress of children in industrial courses.

After five years of intensive study, the committee came to the conclusion that a much more detailed study, with the most modern and reliable methods, was imperative in the schools for the deaf in America.

As a result of recommendation made by the committee, a new survey of schools for the deaf was authorized which was sponsored by the National Research Council. [5] This survey was planned to include all the schools for the deaf that would cooperate. The investigation was begun during the winter of 1924 and was completed in the spring of 1925.

The information which was gathered by the agents of the National Research Council in making the survey covered the following points:

1. Mental and educational measurements.
2. Achievement in speech and speech reading.
3. Degree of residual hearing.
4. Physical features of public Day Schools for the deaf.
5. Physical features of public residential schools or Institutions for the deaf.
6. Management, financial support, and teaching force of Day Schools and Institutions for the deaf.
7. Information regarding age, cause of deafness, age of deafness, nationality, age of starting to school, grade, and length of time spent in school.
8. Nationality, and language spoken most of the time at home by the parents.
9. The father's occupation and the mother's occupation.
10. Industrial courses offered by the schools.

As part of the survey the questionnaire which is reproduced on the next page was filled out for each deaf child twelve years of age or over. On the back of the questionnaire form, provision was made for the record of the scores obtained on the Pintner Non-Language Mental Test, the Pintner Educational Survey Test, the 3 A audiometer score showing the amount of residual hearing for each ear for each child, and the scores gained on the lip-reading and speech tests—which were administered to only the three highest classes in each school because of the necessity of having the sentences composed of words which were familiar to the pupils.

Five reports have been published by the National Research Council concerning the results of the data collected from this survey. These reports raise a number of problems on which the author hopes to throw more light by an intensive study of the material collected by the committee. The study of the problems arising in connection with education of the deaf will be undertaken by contrasting the Day Schools with the Institutions. So great are the differences between the characteristics of these two types of schools for educating the deaf that they must be studied separately. The chapters which follow give ample proof of the desirability of this method of treatment.

SCHOOL............................   DATE........................

PUPIL'S RECORD

[THIS SIDE OF THE CARD IS TO BE FILLED OUT UNDER THE DIRECTION OF
THE HEAD OF THE SCHOOL.]

Name ....Boy or girl ...... Race or color ......
Date of birth (month, day, and year)...............................
Birthplace ....
Age when deafness occurred ....
Cause of deafness ....
Age when first admitted to school ....
Schools for the hearing attended (a) .... (b) ....
Number of years in schools for the hearing............................
Schools for the deaf attended (a) .... (b) ....
Number of years in schools for the deaf ....
Grade of pupil at present ....
Subjects studied by pupil at present (a) .... (b) ....
    (c) .... (d) .... (e) .... (f) ....
    (g) .... (h) .... (i) .... (j) ....
By which of following methods has the pupil been instructed? (If by dif-
ferent methods state how long under each.)
    Oral; auricular; manual alphabet; speech and manual alphabet; manual
    alphabet and sign language; speech, manual alphabet, and sign lan-
    guage ....
Means of communication (writing, speech, lip reading, finger spelling, signs)
    (a) At home .... (b) With teachers .... (c) With
strangers .... (d) With deaf persons ....
Numbers of years taught speech and lip reading......................
Language mainly used at home (English, Italian, Yiddish, etc.) ....
Length of kindergarten training (if any) .... years
Number of years of preliminary manual training ....
Trades learned in school ....
Is home of pupil in country or city? ....
Father—Hearing or deaf .... His birthplace ....
    His occupation ....
Mother—Hearing or deaf .... Her birthplace ....
    Her occupation ....
Are parents blood relatives? ....
General physical condition of pupil (good, fair, or bad).................
    Height .... inches. Weight .... pounds.
With or without shoes and clothing on...............................
    (a) Condition of ears ....
    (b) Condition of eyes .... Are defects, if any, corrected
        by glasses? ....
    (c) Condition of throat ....

CHAPTER III

OUTLINE OF THE DATA AVAILABLE

The following information was made available through the questionnaire which was filled out for each child twelve years of age or older:

1. Chronological age in years and months.
2. Age of starting to school.
3. Age of becoming deaf.
4. Number of years spent in schools for children with normal hearing.
5. Number of years spent in schools for deaf pupils.
6. Language spoken most of the time by the parents.
7. Occupation of the father.

These facts, studied in relation to the test results, should yield important findings about the educational achievements of deaf children in Institutions and Day Schools in America.

Previous studies have indicated that some of these factors have a distinct influence on the educational progress of deaf children. Pintner and Paterson [30], in their study of deaf children, found that the age at which a child became deaf, after four or five years of age, had great influence on the ability of the child to do the tasks required in an examination of educational subject matter, such as Pintner's Educational Survey Test. Reamer [32] found a similar tendency in the children whom she studied, except that she found age six to be the year at which the influence was felt most.

Another important factor determining educational ability is the number of years a child has been in school. This obviously depends, to a large extent, on the chronological age of the child, but the admission requirements in respect to age vary so greatly in the 40 schools studied, that, as will appear later, the number of years a child has attended school is of more importance in determining educational achievement than the actual physical age of the child. The correlation between chronological age and the number of years in a deaf school for 311 cases found in Institutions for the deaf is .56 ± .03. In another sampling of 1,159 cases, also in Institutions for the deaf, the correlation is .56 ± .01. This correlation is lowered somewhat because of the fact that a few of the children have spent part of their educational careers in a school for normal hearing children and, consequently, have been in a school for the deaf a smaller number of years than the children of the same age who have had all their schooling in deaf schools.

The effect that a foreign language spoken most of the time in the home has on educational achievement has not been determined for hearing or deaf children. An analysis of the data available will give some facts about this important topic.*

A fourth influence which can be studied in some detail from the available data is the relationships which exist between social and economic status and educational progress. Two measures of social and economic status are used in this study. Both are based on the occupational status of the father. The first is a 5 to 1 scale used by the Institute of Educational Research, Teachers College, Columbia University. The second is the Barr Scale [34] of Occupational Intelligence. Both are described more fully in Chapter XI.

The three objective tests which were used in this study and which were administered to the deaf children by the field agents of the National Research Council are (1) The Non-Language Group Test of Mental Ability by Pintner [26], (2) the Educational Survey Test by Pintner [27], and (3) a test of residual hearing by means of the 3 A audiometer [7].

The manner in which the third test was given to the children is described in the following terms: "The hearing of each ear was tested some 8 or 10 times before a decision was reached, and every precaution was taken to prevent error in the results." [9] This excerpt shows the care that was taken to render the results as reliable as possible.

The agents of the National Research Council made the greatest possible efforts to secure a representative sampling of deaf children in the United States. [9] After many months of negotiations 42 schools from every group of states in the Union offered their

* See Chapter X.

coöperation. It was decided that all children in these schools, twelve years of age and over, should be included in the survey. This program was adhered to, with the result that more than 4,000 children in these schools were included in the investigation. Among the schools for the deaf two distinct kinds may be distinguished: the Day School and the Institution. The Day School, as its name implies, admits children for the day only. Their lodging and food is supplied by parents or guardians. On the other hand, the children who attend Institutions spend the whole twenty-four hours there. During the past half-century there has been considerable discussion about the value of the Day School. Several schools for the deaf have committed themselves to the practice of being Day Schools from the beginning, but the majority of schools for the deaf are of the Institutional type. It has been felt that the handicap suffered by the deaf is such that it can be overcome only by continuous contact with the teachers. The relatively few hours spent in class in a Day School is considered far from sufficient for the most rapid advancement. [3] The discussion concerning which type of school is better has received much attention but, until the survey was made by the National Research Council there was available relatively little definite information based on experimental investigation.

From his studies Pintner reports: "The Residential schools are loaded with poorer mental material as contrasted with the day schools. The residential schools have more backward and dull. There are three times the percentage of dull in the residential as compared with the day schools." [23]

Another authority [9] reports that the Day Schools attract pupils with a greater average degree of residual hearing than the Institutions.

Some of the questions which remain to be answered and on which light will be thrown by this study are suggested by the authorities referred to: Is the factor of residual hearing an important explanation for the apparently poor caliber of pupil who attends the residential school or—as it is called in this study— the Institutional School? If children of the same age and mental ability were found in the Day Schools and the Institutions, would the Day Schools still produce better educational achievement?

In the chapters which follow, the two types of schools will

be treated separately and then contrasted. In all possible cases a statistical evaluation of the significance of the differences found will be given.

As reported by the National Research Council [23], measurements of and information about more than 4,000 children in 42 Day Schools and Institutions for the deaf were obtained. Not all the information and measurements, however, were available for each child. For purposes of more exact comparison, it was thought desirable to use only those children who had complete records. It was necessary, therefore, to eliminate all cases whose records were incomplete or inaccurate for the variables reported earlier in this chapter.

Some of the records were found to contain palpable errors in the numerical information. A check was possible in that the age of starting to school plus the number of years spent in a deaf school plus the number of years spent in a hearing school should equal the age of the child. If the total did not tally, the record was eliminated on the assumption that a mistake had been made or that sickness, travel, or some other cause interrupted the continuity of the child's education. When the records showing discrepancies had been eliminated there remained 316 complete records for Day School children and 1,470 complete records for Institutional children.

Inasmuch as the influence of language spoken at home and the occupation of the father could not be determined by the same procedures as were used for the other variables, records which showed these incomplete were not rejected if the other eight variables were present and accurate.

The central theme of this study may now be outlined in the following terms: The P.N.L.* test and the audiometer test, together with the seven items of information gained from the questionnaire, make up the factors which will be studied for their effect on educational progress and achievement, as measured by the Pintner Educational Survey Test, in (1) the Day Schools for the deaf and (2) the Institutions for the deaf. The similarities and differences between these two types of schools for the deaf will be stressed.

* The letters P.N.L. in this study refer to the Pintner Non-Language Group Test of Mental Ability.

CHAPTER IV

STUDY OF THE SAMPLING OF CHILDREN INVESTIGATED

In the preceding chapter it was stated that the National Research Council made every possible effort to obtain a representative sampling of the pupils in the Day Schools and Institutions for the deaf. Before any results of the present investigation are reported it is important to determine to what extent the data used are a random sampling of deaf children in the United States. As has already been stated, an attempt was made to study all the children in each school who were twelve years of age or older.

In the *American Annals of the Deaf* [23], Pintner compares the percentages of deaf children studied in each of the nine large subdivisions into which the United States is divided by the United States Census, 1920 [6], with those found in the census.

It was essential to find out if the process of eliminating the cases having incomplete or inaccurate records would markedly disturb the percentages in each division. In Table 1 the final column gives the percentage of all the 1,786 cases used in this study which are to be found in each division.

It is evident from the table that the process of selection has changed very few of the percentages from those found when the total number of cases is used. The only difference apparent is the increase of the percentage of children used from the Middle Atlantic States. This percentage, already larger than that found by the census, is slightly increased. (This may suggest a more accurate and thorough investigation of the school children in the Middle Atlantic States than in the Pacific and South Atlantic States.) All the differences, however, are small. In general, the distribution of cases used in this study is the same as the distribution of deaf people throughout the United States. The two sections where this is least true are the Middle Atlantic States, which contain 37 per cent of the cases used in this study as contrasted with 18.6 per cent of all deaf people, and the East North Central States, which contain only 12.9 per cent of the cases in this study as contrasted with 24 per cent of all deaf people. Figure I shows graphically the results tabulated in Table 1. The agreement for seven of the nine geographic divisions is remarkably close.

TABLE 1

SUMMARY BY GEOGRAPHICAL LOCATION OF DEAF IN (1) UNITED STATES, 1920 CENSUS, (2) NATIONAL RESEARCH COUNCIL SURVEY, AND (3) THIS STUDY

Geographical Division	1920 Census		National Research Council		This Study	
	No.	Per Cent	No.	Per Cent	No.	Per Cent
Pacific	2,045	4.6	282	6.4	62	3.5
Mountain	1,211	2.7	174	3.9	52	2.9
West South Central	3,902	8.7	456	10.3	204	11.4
East South Central	3,745	8.3	404	9.1	175	9.8
South Atlantic	5,946	13.2	540	12.2	171	9.6
West North Central	5,812	12.9	506	11.4	171	9.6
East North Central	10,770	24.0	488	11.0	230	12.9
Middle Atlantic	8,361	18.6	1,426	32.2	661	37.0
New England	3,093	6.9	156	3.5	60	3.4
Total	44,885	99.9	4,432	100.	1786	100.1

In order to ascertain whether the eliminated cases fell among the older children or the brighter children, comparison was made of the means and the sigmas of the cases which were not used with the means and sigmas of the cases used in this study. Table 2 gives this information.

The mean chronological age of the Day School groups of 311 cases is the same as the Day School group of 336 unused cases. There is a difference of 1.23 in the sigmas. The mean for the 1,470 cases which were used from the Institutions is one month lower than the mean for the 1,403 cases which were not used. The variability of the two groups is the same. There is, then, no important difference in chronological age between the cases used and those rejected.

FIGURE I. GEOGRAPHIC DISTRIBUTIONS OF DEAF PUPILS STUDIED

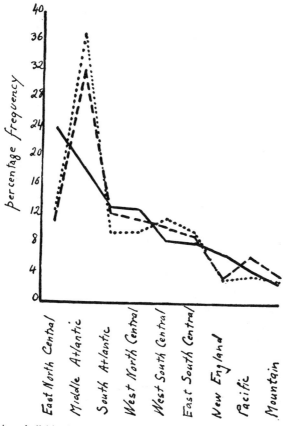

——— % in each division in Census, 1920.
- - - - % in each division in National Research Council Survey.
· · · · % in each division in this study.

When the mental ratings of the groups are compared there seems to be some difference. Between the two Day School groups there is a difference of 14.1 and between the two Institutional groups there is a difference of 6.65. In both comparisons the variability of the group not included is greater than the variability of the group that was included in this study. It is probable that the consistency of the differences indicates a true difference, although neither of the differences between the means is statistically significant, as is shown by the data of Table 3.

TABLE 2

COMPARISON OF DEAF SAMPLING USED IN THIS STUDY WITH SAMPLING RE-
JECTED IN RESPECT TO CHRONOLOGICAL AGE AND PINTNER
NON-LANGUAGE SCORE, AGES 12 TO 17 INCLUSIVE

	Day School		Institution	
	Used	Not Used	Used	Not Used
Chronological Age				
Mean	14–6½	14–6	14–11	15–0
S. D.	19.09	17.86	19.62	19.61
P. N. L. Score				
Mean	340.9	326.8	304.15	297.5
S. D.	99.57	110.85	119.00	125.13

There are 95 chances in 100 * that the difference of 14.1 obtained between the Day School groups is significant and 92 chances in 100 that the 6.65 obtained between the Institutional groups is significant. In order to be practically certain that a difference is significant there must be 99.9 chances in 100 that the obtained difference is above zero. [19]

TABLE 3

SIGNIFICANCE OF DIFFERENCES FOUND BETWEEN THE "USED" AND "UN-
USED" CASES IN RESPECT TO P. N. L. SCORE IN THE DAY SCHOOLS AND
IN THE INSTITUTIONS

	Used Cases S. D_{M1}	Unused Cases S. D_{M2}	S. $D_{diff.}$	Diff.	$\dfrac{\text{Diff.}}{\text{S. } D_{diff.}}$
Day Schools	6.64	5.66	8.72	14.10	1.62
Institutions	3.60	3.11	4.76	6.65	1.40

In this study only the cases between twelve and seventeen years of age inclusive were included. This selection was somewhat arbitrary but was based on the fact that, after the age of about eighteen years, many children had been graduated, leaving a selected group whose schooling had been irregular, who were below their companions in mental ability, or who had not started to school until relatively late in life.

* See Appendix I.

It seems fair, then, to conclude that the cases studied are representative of all the cases for whom the National Research Council gathered data. In general, the cases included in this study are distributed over the United States in a manner similar to the total deaf population. The results obtained, therefore, should be indicative of what would be obtained if all the children in Day Schools and Institutions for the deaf had been studied.

CHAPTER V

COMPARISON OF MATCHED CASES FROM
DAY SCHOOLS AND INSTITUTIONS

Best gives the chief argument in favor of the Institution as the superior type of school environment for the deaf, in the following terms: "In the institution the children may be under intelligent supervision and direction their entire time, and they may be able to get, outside of school hours, a part of the education which the hearing child so naturally acquires, for, in an institution, learning continues outside the classroom as well as within." [3] Logically, then, one would expect that children in the Institutions would have progressed more, educationally, than children who go to Day Schools for only a few hours each day. However, Pintner [23], in his analysis of the data collected by the National Research Council, finds that such is not the case. The average Day School child secures a higher educational score than the average Institutional child. This remains true for absolute score and when the factor of age is made constant for the two groups. Pintner points out that part of this difference in favor of the Day School is to be expected, since the Day School draws children with greater mental ability. This chapter will show, among other things, how significant this difference is statistically. It will also evaluate the differences found between the other variables reported by the National Research Council which have been enumerated previously.

In the Day Schools 316 cases were found to have complete and accurate records and in the Institutions 1,470 cases had complete and accurate records, according to the standards previously described. Of the 316 cases in the Day Schools, five had to be rejected because it was not possible to match them with cases who had similar records from the Institution. There were, therefore, nearly five times as many cases available in the Institutions as in the Day Schools. Table 4 shows the distribution of

16

the 311 Day School pupils, and the 1,470 children in the Institutions, according to their scores on the Pintner Non-Language Test of Mental Ability.

Figure II gives this information graphically. The differences between the two groups in average score and in spread are easily seen from this figure. The Institutions have greater percentages in the lower levels of mental ability and also in the two highest levels but smaller percentages in the middle and upper middle. This figure illustrates the facts reported by Pintner.

Table 5 and Figure III give distributions for the Pintner Educational Survey Test. In this test the average Institutional child receives a score 12.1 points lower than the average Day School child. There is, contrary to what appeared on the P. N. L. Test, greater dispersion among the Day School pupils. Figure III,

TABLE 4

DISTRIBUTION OF CHILDREN IN THE P. N. L. TEST IN THE DAY SCHOOLS AND
INSTITUTIONS

P. N. L. Score	Day Schools		Institutions	
	Frequency	Per Cent	Frequency	Per Cent
595	..	..	1	.0
560	1	.3	7	.5
525	4	1.3	19	1.3
490	14	4.5	45	3.1
455	20	6.4	64	4.4
420	30	9.7	116	7.9
385	37	11.9	143	9.7
350	51	16.4	150	10.2
315	37	11.9	172	11.7
280	33	10.6	185	12.6
245	30	9.7	132	9.0
210	19	6.1	115	7.8
175	16	5.1	94	6.4
140	12	3.9	76	5.2
105	4	1.3	52	3.5
70	2	.6	50	3.4
35	0	..	27	1.8
0	1	.3	22	1.5
Number	311	100.0	1,470	100.0
Mean	340.9		304.2	
S. D.	99.6		119.0	

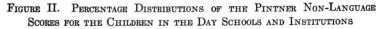

FIGURE II. PERCENTAGE DISTRIBUTIONS OF THE PINTNER NON-LANGUAGE
SCORES FOR THE CHILDREN IN THE DAY SCHOOLS AND INSTITUTIONS

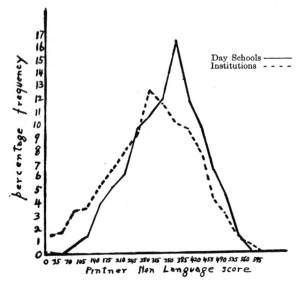

however, suggests that this may be due to the relatively large
number of scores between zero and 5.99 among the Institutional
children. The test was evidently too difficult for this group of
children. The test was too difficult for a smaller percentage of
Day School children.

From Figures II and III naturally arises the question of the
effect upon the Educational Survey Test curves of making the
curves of mental ability coincide. The following procedure was
chosen in order to answer this question.

In the previous analysis of these data, no attempt was made
to compare children in Day Schools and those in Institutions
with the same mental ability, although Pintner made a comparison of the mental and educational indices of the two groups and
found that the Day Schools, according to the Educational Survey Test, were accomplishing more in relation to the mental
ability of their children than the Institutions. The significance
of this difference was not determined.

In order that neither Day Schools nor Institutions should
have any superiority in regard to native intelligence, the children in the Day Schools were matched with Institutional children

TABLE 5

DISTRIBUTION OF CHILDREN ON THE PINTNER EDUCATIONAL SURVEY TEST
IN THE DAY SCHOOLS AND INSTITUTIONS

Survey Test Score	Day Schools		Institutions	
	Frequency	Per Cent	Frequency	Per Cent
108	..	..	1	.0
102	..	..	0	.0
96	3	1.0	3	.2
90	2	.6	1	.0
84	3	1.0	5	.3
78	6	1.9	7	.5
72	9	2.9	11	.8
66	10	3.2	11	.8
60	12	3.9	21	1.4
54	19	6.1	31	2.1
48	19	6.1	55	3.7
42	23	7.4	58	3.9
36	28	9.0	92	6.3
30	35	11.3	125	8.5
24	33	10.6	164	11.2
18	36	11.6	202	13.7
12	22	7.1	240	16.3
6	32	10.3	241	16.4
0—5.9	19	6.1	202	13.7
Number	311	100.1	1,470	99.8
Mean	35.4		23.3	
S. D.	22.1		17.5	

of the same mental ability, as measured by the Pintner Non-Language Test. In addition to the factor of mentality, it was thought necessary to have children of the same age so that a fair comparison of their educational achievement might be made. Thus, by matching each Day School child with an Institutional child of similar age and intelligence, the two most important factors in the educational achievement and progress of hearing children were made constant.

An arbitrary measure of similarity was established. Two children whose scores on the Non-Language Test were within twenty points of each other were considered as having the same intelligence rating. Two children whose ages were within four months of each other were considered as having similar ages.

FIGURE III. PERCENTAGE DISTRIBUTIONS OF THE PINTNER SURVEY SCORES
FOR THE CHILDREN IN THE DAY SCHOOLS AND INSTITUTIONS

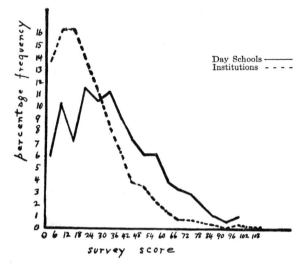

When these tests were applied to the 316 Day School cases
and the 1,470 Institutional cases, it was found that all but five
of the Day School cases could be matched with Institutional
cases. Thus 311 pairs of children were available for study. The
children in each pair were equal in mental ability and age. The
manner and significance of their variation in other respects will
now be considered.

The extent to which the two groups coincide in scores on the
Non-Language Test and in chronological age is given in dia-
grammatic form in Figure IV and Figure V. It will be noted that
the lines indicating the two groups nearly coincide at all points
for both mental ability and chronological age. Another form of
presenting the closeness of this matching is by a comparison of
the means and sigmas of the two groups. The difference of the
means is found, and the significance of this difference is computed by dividing the difference by the sigma of the difference.[*]
Table 6 gives this information for chronological age and for
Pintner Non-Language Test.

* This technique is used very frequently in this study. It will be assumed that if the
ratio $\dfrac{\text{difference}}{\text{S.D. [diff.]}}$ equals or exceeds 3.0 the difference is significant. A ratio of 3.0 indicates
that there are 999 chance in 1,000 that the true difference between the variables will be
greater than zero in the direction of the obtained difference. See Appendix I.

FIGURE IV. DISTRIBUTIONS OF THE P.N.L. TEST SCORES FOR THE 311 DAY SCHOOL CASES AND THE MATCHED 311 INSTITUTIONAL CASES

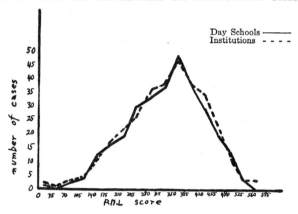

FIGURE V. DISTRIBUTIONS OF CHRONOLOGICAL AGES FOR THE 311 DAY SCHOOL CASES AND THE MATCHED 311 INSTITUTIONAL CASES

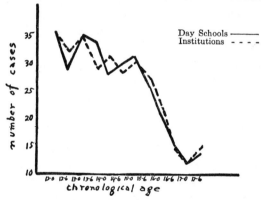

The ratio of .12 for chronological age is an altogether negligible difference. There are 41 chances in one hundred that the true difference is not greater than zero. The ratio .07 for scores on the Pintner Non-Language Test reveals an even less reliable difference, there being about 47 chances in one hundred that the true difference is not greater than zero. The evidence, from both the graphic and the numerical methods of comparison, reveals very slight differences between the Day School group and the Institutional group in regard to the factors of mental ability and age. Differences found between the two groups on educa-

TABLE 6

INSIGNIFICANCE OF DIFFERENCES OBTAINED AFTER MATCHING 311 PAIRS
OF DAY SCHOOL AND INSTITUTIONAL CHILDREN

Variable	Mean	S. D.	S. D.M	Diff.	S. D.diff.	$\dfrac{\text{Diff.}}{\text{S. D.diff.}}$
Chronological Age						
Day Schools ...	14 yrs. 6.54	19.09	1.08			
Institutions	14 yrs. 6.35	19.12	1.08	.19	1.53	.12
P. N. L. Score						
Day Schools ...	340.90	99.57	5.66			
Institutions	341.49	99.34	5.64	.59	7.99	.07

tional achievement will be due to the type of school they attend
plus the influence of other factors, for some of the most important of which numerical information is available. Table 7 gives
the means, sigmas, and sigmas of the means of the following
variables for both the Day Schools and the Institutions:

1. Pintner Educational Survey Test score.
2. Maximum Audiometer score.
3. Years spent in a school for deaf children.
4. Years spent in a school for children with normal hearing.
5. Age of starting to school.
6. Age of becoming deaf.

Table 7 also gives the differences between the Day School and
the Institution for each variable, the sigmas of these differences,
the difference divided by the sigma of the difference, and the
chances in 100 that the true difference is greater than zero.

The mean score for the Pintner Survey Test in Institutions is
10.08 points lower than the mean score for the Pintner Educational Survey Test in the Day Schools. Thus, when those children
in the Institutions are selected who are comparable with the Day
School children in age and in mental ability, the Day School
pupils show more progress than the pupils in the Institution.

Is this difference of 10.08 points a chance difference; that is,
if another sampling were taken, would the difference disappear
or be in favor of the Institution? This question may be answered
from Table 7. There are 100 chances out of 100 that the true

difference is above zero. There is no doubt that the difference is significant between the two types of schools in regard to accomplishment on the Pintner Educational Survey Test. Expressed a little differently, there are 99.9 chances in 100 that the true difference will never fall below 10.08 $\pm$ 3 (1.62); that is, below 5.22.

But from these results alone it would not be safe to conclude that the teaching in the Day Schools is more efficient than that in Institutions, or that the Day School methods secure better results than those employed in the Institutions. Several factors besides mental ability and chronological age affect the scores obtained on the Educational Survey Test.

TABLE 7

SIGNIFICANCE OF DIFFERENCES OBTAINED BETWEEN THE DAY SCHOOLS AND THE INSTITUTIONS* IN THE VARIABLES INDICATED

Variable	Mean	S. D.	S. D.$_M$	Diff.	S. D.$_{diff.}$	$\dfrac{\text{Diff.}}{\text{S. D.}_{diff.}}$	Chances in 100 That Diff. Is Significant
Survey Test Score							
Day Schools ..	35.40	22.05	1.30				
Institutions ..	25.32	17.02	.96	10.08	1.62	6.2	100
Audiometer Maximum Score							
Day Schools ..	37.80	21.42	1.23				
Institutions ..	29.10	16.50	.94	8.70	1.55	5.6	100
Years in Schools for Deaf							
Day Schools ..	6.29	3.02	1.71				
Institutions ..	7.26	2.43	1.37	.97	.22	4.4	100
Years in Schools for Hearing							
Day Schools ..	1.98	2.45	.14				
Institutions ..	.69	.93	.05	1.29	.15	8.7	100
Age of Starting to School							
Day Schools ..	7.19	1.77	.10				
Institutions ..	7.69	1.80	.10	.50	.14	3.5	100
Age of Becoming Deaf							
Day Schools ..	2.69	2.88	.16				
Institutions ..	1.52	1.76	.10	1.17	.19	6.2	100

* The number of cases is 311.

One factor which has been frequently found to influence educational progress is that of the age of becoming deaf. Table 7 shows that the mean age of becoming deaf among Day School children is two years and about eight months, and among the children in Institutions the mean age is one year and six months—a difference of a year and two months. Not only is the mean age of becoming deaf less in the Institutions than in the Day Schools, but there is also a smaller variability. That is,

FIGURE VI. DIFFERENCE BETWEEN THE DAY SCHOOLS AND INSTITUTIONS IN
FREQUENCY AT EACH AGE OF BECOMING DEAF

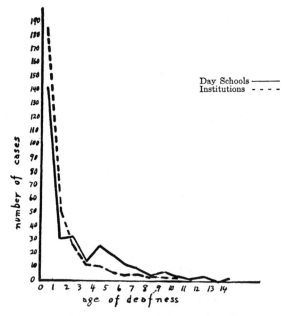

the range of ages of becoming deaf is greater than among the children of the Day Schools. Figure VI illustrates the differences between the Day Schools and the Institutions for each age of becoming deaf. Of children who were born deaf or became deaf before their first birthday, 77 per cent are in the Institutions and 66 per cent are in the Day Schools. On the other hand, for every age level above two years, the Day Schools contain a greater percentage than the Institutions. The effect which this difference has on educational progress is not revealed by this comparison, but there are 100 chances in 100 that the difference is significant.

Still another factor has been thought to affect the rate of learning of deaf children: the amount of residual hearing possessed. Table 7 gives the comparison of the Day Schools and the Institutions in this respect. (The measure of residual hearing used in this study is not the average residual hearing of the two ears, but the maximum degree of hearing recorded for the child. Thus, if a child's right ear was credited with 50 per cent of normal hearing and the left 20 per cent the score of 50 was used.) The difference of 8.70 points between the pupils of the two types of schools is highly reliable, there being 99.9 chances in 100 that the true difference would not fall below 4.05 points. It is certain that the Day Schools represented in this survey draw children with a relatively greater degree of residual hearing than do the Institutions. Again, the effect that this additional hearing has on school achievement is not clear.

Another factor which may have an effect on the educational score when age is kept constant is the age of beginning school. The children who attend the Day Schools for the deaf started to school a little earlier than those who attend the Institutions. The difference revealed here is .50 years. There seems to be no great variation in the dispersion of the two groups. Both have approximately the same standard deviations. Again, the question arises as to the significance of this difference. The probabilities are fewer than 9 in 10,000 that the true difference between the Day Schools and the Institutions in this variable is zero. There is practical certainty that the Day Schools allow children to start to school earlier than do the Institutions.

From Figure VI it may be seen that more children in the Day School group became deaf after five years of age than in the Institutional group. Actually, 61 children in the 311 Day School cases became deaf during their fifth year or later. In the Institutional group only 20 became deaf during the fifth year or later. In other words, 20 per cent of the pupils in the Day Schools as compared with 6 per cent in the Institutions became deaf in their fifth year. Since children may begin school as early as five years, it is to be expected that the children in the Day School have attended schools for the hearing for a longer period than the children in the Institutions. Table 7 proves this to be the case.

The difference of 1 year and 4 months is highly reliable, there being 99.9 chances in 100 that the true difference will not fall below .84 of a year or about 10 months. As was expected, the Day School children have attended a school for children with normal hearing for a longer period than the children from the Institutions. Since 20 per cent of the Day School pupils lost their hearing during their fifth year or later it is probable that many of the children profited greatly from the period spent in a normal school. Naturally, the tendency would be to raise the average educational score for the Day School group.

On the other hand, the children in the Institutions have, on the average, spent more time in a school for the deaf than have the children in the Day Schools. The mean number of years that these 311 children in the Institutions spent in a deaf school is 7.26; that of the 311 Day School pupils 6.29. The difference of .97 years is significant, there being 99.9 chances in 100 that the true difference will not fall below .31 of a year or 4 months.

But it may be noted that the difference of the sigmas of the difference of years in the school for the deaf is not so great as the difference of years in the schools for the hearing. This is explained by the fact previously found that the Day School children start to school earlier in life than the Institutional cases, and in these groups the chronological age is constant.

The findings reported in this chapter may be summarized as follows:

1. The Day School pupils, when paired with Institutional children of the same age and intelligence, have a marked advantage in the average score on the Educational Survey Test.

2. This superiority in educational achievement is accompanied by a superiority in the following factors, some of which are thought to influence educational achievement to considerable extent.

    (a) Age of becoming deaf.

    (b) Degree of residual hearing.

    (c) Age of starting school.

    (d) Years spent in a school for normal hearing children.

    (e) Total number of years in school.

3. Institutional children have been in schools for the deaf for a greater number of years than Day School pupils.

So far, no final statement can be made about the relative merits of the teaching in the two types of schools, as measured by the Pintner Educational Survey Test.

CHAPTER VI

OBTAINED DIFFERENCES

In this chapter a study will be made of the differences between the various groups into which the 1,781 cases have been divided. Chapter V showed the differences between the Day School pupils and an equal number from the Institutions matched for age and mental ability. The next comparison will be between the 311 cases from the Institutions and the 1,159 cases which remain. Another comparison will be made between the Day School pupils and the entire 1,470 cases in the Institutions; and finally a comparison will be made between the 311 cases from the Institutions and the entire group of 1,470.

Table 8 shows the means and sigmas for each of the variables, for the group of 311 cases from the Institutions and for the group of 1,159 cases. The differences between the two groups are also given for both the means and the sigmas. The unselected group of 1,159 started to school a half year later than the selected

TABLE 8

MEANS AND SIGMAS WITH THEIR DIFFERENCES, FOR THE GROUP OF 311 CASES FROM THE INSTITUTIONS AND THE GROUP OF 1,159

Variable	Mean			S. D.		
	311	1,159 Institutional Cases	Diff.	311	1,159 Institutional Cases	Diff.
C. A.	14–6.34	15–0.40	+ 6.06	19.12	19.54	+.42
P. N. L. Score	341.495	294.14	−47.355	99.34	121.94	+22.60
Survey Test Score	25.32	22.84	− 2.48	17.02	17.59	+.57
Audiometer Maximum	29.10 ·	28.21	−.89	16.50	16.72	+.22
Years in Schools for Deaf ..	7.26	7.205	−.065	2.43	2.57	+.14
Years in Schools for Hearing.	.693	.654	−.039	.928	.913	−.15
Age of Starting to School ..	7.69	8.214	+.524	1.796	2.009	+.213
Age of Becoming Deaf	1.52	1.47	−.05	1.765	1.73	−.053

27

group and are, on the average, six months older. The selected group of 311 cases scored better on the Pintner Non-Language Test and on the Pintner Rapid Survey Test. The children of this group have little more residual hearing and become deaf a trifle earlier. They have been in school a little longer. Table 9 gives the differences referred to above, the sigmas of these differences, the ratios of the difference to the sigma of the difference and the chances in 100 that the obtained differences are significant. In three items the differences are statistically reliable; that is in chronological age, age of starting to school, and mental ability. The difference between the two in educational achievement is relatively reliable, there being 99 chances in 100 that the true difference is above zero. The other differences can be readily accounted for by chance. The reliably greater age of the 1,159 Institutional children and their reliably poorer Pintner Non-Language Test score makes the group of 1,159 cases markedly below the group of 311 in mental ability. In terms of intelligence quotients there would be even more difference between the groups than is shown by the P. N. L. score alone. This should have the effect of giving the selected cases a higher educational score than the unselected group. This expectation is fulfilled, but the difference does not attain absolute reliability. Other things being equal, a greater difference would have been

TABLE 9

SIGNIFICANCE OF DIFFERENCES BETWEEN THE MATCHED INSTITUTIONAL GROUP OF 311 CHILDREN AND THE 1,159 CHILDREN WHO COMPOSE THE REST OF THE GROUP

Variable	Difference Between Inst. 311 and Inst. 1,159	S. D.Diff.	$\frac{\text{Diff.}}{\text{S. D.Diff.}}$	Chances in 100 That Difference Is Significant
C. A.	6.06	1.23	4.9	100
P. N. L. Score	47.35	6.63	7.1	100
Survey Test Score	2.48	1.10	2.3	99
Audiometer Maximum	.89	1.05	.8	79
Years in Schools for Deaf	.06	.15	.4	65
Years in Schools for Hearing	.04	.06	.7	76
Age of Starting to School	.52	.12	4.4	100
Age of Becoming Deaf	.05	.11	.0	50

predicted. It is possible that these young bright children are not encouraged to accomplish as much as they can when they constitute a minority in their classes. This hypothesis cannot be checked from the data at hand.

The effect on the Educational Survey Test score of the fact that the selected group started to school earlier than the unselected cannot be estimated at present. The absence of a significant difference between the two groups in the amount of time spent in school would indicate that the difference in chronological age is due to the fact of starting to school later. However, the very significant difference between the two groups in mental ability would suggest a relationship between mental backwardness and time of starting to school. As will be shown later, there is a substantial negative correlation between these two variables for each of the groups studied. It is several points higher for the 1,159 unselected cases. This may be due to the greater variability of the 1,159 group in P. N. L. score (sigma for 1,159 cases on the P.N.L. is 121.94; sigma of the selected group of 311 on the P.N.L. is 99.34).

Table 10 gives the chances in 100 that the differences between the selected group of 311 cases and the entire group of 1,470 cases are significant. The three differences which were reliable when the 1,159 cases were compared with the 311 cases are still reliable. There is one chance in every 25 that the difference between

TABLE 10

SIGNIFICANCE OF DIFFERENCES BETWEEN THE GROUP OF 311 CASES FROM THE INSTITUTIONS AND THE WHOLE INSTITUTIONAL GROUP

Variable	Difference Between 311 and 1,470 Cases	S. D.Diff.	Diff. / S. D.Diff.	Chances in 100 That Difference Is Significant
C. A.	4.66	1.19	3.9	100
P. N. L. Score	37.35	6.44	5.8	100
Survey Test Score	1.98	1.07	1.8	96
Audiometer Maximum	.72	1.04	.7	76
Years in Schools for Deaf	.04	.15	.3	62
Years in Schools for Hearing	.03	.06	.5	69
Age of Starting to School	.41	.11	3.6	100
Age of Becoming Deaf	.04	.11	.3	62

the two groups in educational achievement will be zero. This difference is considerably less reliable than the difference obtained when the 1,159 cases were compared with the 311 cases. All the other differences lack statistical significance.

Table 11 gives the chances in 100 that the Day Schools really differ from the Institutions in each of the eight variables. There is absolute certainty that the two types of schools draw children who, in general, differ widely from one another in each of the variables in which they have been measured. For every variable there are 100 chances out of 100 that the true difference would not fall as low as zero.

TABLE 11

SIGNIFICANCE OF DIFFERENCES BETWEEN THE DAY SCHOOLS AND THE TOTAL GROUP OF INSTITUTIONS

Variable	Difference Between Day School Group and 1,470 Cases from Institution	S. D.Diff.	Diff. / S. D.Diff.	Chances in 100 That Difference Is Significant
C. A.	4.46	1.20	3.8	100
P. N. L. Score	36.75	6.44	5.7	100
Survey Test Score	12.08	1.33	9.1	100
Audiometer Maximum	9.42	1.29	7.3	100
Years in Schools for Deaf	.93	.16	6.0	100
Years in Schools for Hearing	1.32	.14	9.4	100
Age of Starting to School	.91	.11	8.1	100
Age of Becoming Deaf	1.21	.17	7.1	100

Table 12 summarizes the data that have been presented so far in regard to the significance of the differences in the variables under consideration for the following four groups:

1. Day School and 311 cases selected from the Institutions.
2. Day School and the entire group from the Institutions.
3. Selected group from the Institutions and the rest of the cases.
4. Selected group from the Institutions and the entire group.

This summary shows clearly that the Day Schools and the Institutions cater to children who, on the average, are very unlike in their capacities to do the tasks required in gaining an education. These findings, which show how distinct the average child in the Day School is from the average child in the Institution, should be emphasized in comparisons between the results obtained in the two types of schools in order that due allowance may be made for the difficulties encountered by the teachers and principals of the Institutions in educating the children entrusted to their care.

TABLE 12

COMPARISON OF THE RATIOS OF DIFFERENCE TO S. D. OF DIFFERENCE FOR:
(1) DAY SCHOOL GROUP AND MATCHED CASES FOR THE INSTITUTIONS,
(2) DAY SCHOOL GROUP AND TOTAL GROUP OF INSTITUTIONAL CASES,
(3) MATCHED CASES FOR THE INSTITUTIONS AND THE REST OF THE
INSTITUTIONAL CASES, AND (4) MATCHED CASES FROM THE INSTITUTIONS AND THE TOTAL INSTITUTIONAL GROUP.

Variable	311 Cases in Day Schools and 311 in Institutions	311 Cases in Day Schools and 1,470 in Institutions	311 Selected Cases and 1,159 Cases in Institutions	311 Selected Cases and Total of 1,470 Cases in Institutions
C. A.	.1	3.8	4.9	3.9
P. N. L. Score	.1	5.7	7.1	5.8
Survey Test Score	6.2	9.1	2.3	1.8
Audiometer Maximum	5.6	7.3	.8	.7
Years in Schools for the Deaf ...	4.4	6.0	.4	.3
Years in Schools for the Hearing .	8.7	9.4	.7	.5
Age of Starting to School	3.5	8.1	4.4	3.6
Age of Becoming Deaf	6.2	7.1	.0	.3

Table 12 shows the variables in which the 311 selected cases seem representative of the entire group and those in which the process of selection created distinct differences. In residual hearing, years spent in a school for the deaf, years spent in a school for hearing children, and the age of becoming deaf, the 311 cases are relatively similar to the whole group. In chronological age, mental ability, and age of starting to school the influence of selection is noted. So far, only the differences between the means have been considered. Some consideration must now be given to the differences in variability.

Table 13 gives the standard deviations for each of the variables in the two types of schools, and the coefficients of variation

TABLE 13

Coefficients of Variation and S. D.'s for Each of the Variables in the Day Schools and the Institutions

Variable	Day Schools		Institutions	
	V	S. D.	V	S. D.
C. A.	11	19.09	11	19.62
P. N. L. Score	29	99.57	39	119.00
Survey Test Score	62	22.05	75	17.52
Audiometer Maximum	57	21.42	59	16.68
Years in Schools for Deaf	48	3.02	35	2.54
Years in Schools for Hearing	122	2.45	139	.92
Age of Starting to School	25	1.77	24	1.98
Age of Becoming Deaf	107	2.88	116	1.74

of the variables in each type of school. The coefficient of variation [16], symbolized by the letter V, gives a measure of variability independent of the size of the units of measurement used, but relative to the size of the mean, thus permitting comparisons between variables which are measured by different units. Table 13 shows a very wide range of coefficients of variation from 11 in chronological age to 139 in years spent in a school for the hearing by Institutional children.

As measured by V, the variability of the Educational Survey Test, years spent in a school for hearing children, and age of becoming deaf for pupils of the Day Schools is less than that for pupils in Institutions. The standard deviations show the opposite tendency. The coefficients of variation for the Educational Survey Test in both the Institutions and the Day Schools are approximately twice the size of the coefficients of variation for the Pintner Non-Language Test. In other words, the variability in educational achievement is twice that of mental ability. This is as one would expect, because educational achievement is dependent not only on mental ability but also on a large number of other factors, such as age of becoming deaf and degree of residual hearing. It is doubtful if the coefficient of variation should be used with chronological age and age of starting to school. In both of these the zero point of the scale is not zero for these groups but a point more or less arbitrarily fixed considerably above zero. Comparisons between the coefficients of variation for either of these variables with coefficients of variation for the others will lead to erroneous conclusions.

If we exclude these two traits, there is a higher variability in the Institutions for the Pintner Non-Language Test, the Pintner Educational Survey Test, years spent in a school for hearing children, and age of becoming deaf. There is little difference in maximum degree of residual hearing. Only in years spent in a school for the deaf does the variability of the Day Schools exceed that of the Institutions. When the size of the mean is made constant by means of the coefficient of variation the Day Schools are shown to select their children more rigidly than the Institutions.

CHAPTER VII

NEED FOR COMPARISON OF MORE NEARLY COMPARABLE GROUPS

The facts which have been considered up to this point suggest certain other problems which are very important for a full understanding of the education of the deaf.

1. What contribution does each of the variables studied make towards achievement on the Educational Survey Test?

2. What contribution does an increase of a given number of points on the Pintner Non-Language Test make towards an increase of score on the Educational Survey Test?

3. Does this contribution vary at different points of the total scale which runs from 0 to 600?

4. What contribution towards an increase in the score on the Educational Survey Test is made by a given unit of increase in residual hearing?

Some attention will now be devoted to the influence exerted by given units of certain variables on increases in Educational Survey Test score. This section will throw some light on the first of the problems stated above.

The increase in Educational Survey Test score that accompanies given increases in age of becoming deaf is shown in Table 14 and in Figure VIII both for the Day School group and for the entire Institutional group. There appears a gradual increase in Educational Survey Test score for each additional two years of hearing that the children have enjoyed up to the age of six. This is true in both Day Schools and Institutions. The small decrease in the Survey Test score for the ages of six and seven in the Day Schools is probably not significant. Those who became deaf at eight years of age, or afterward, have a very pronounced advantage on the Educational Survey Test. This confirms what has been previously found by Pintner and Paterson and by Reamer.

34

TABLE 14

INCREASES IN EDUCATIONAL SCORES AS AGE OF BECOMING DEAF INCREASES

Age of Becoming Deaf	Median Survey Test Score		Number of Cases	
	Day Schools	Institutions	Day Schools	Institutions
8 or more	52	60	21	16
6 or 7	38	30	20	36
4 or 5	40	27	46	70
2 or 3	31	22	47	224
0 or 1	28	18	177	1124

Table 15 and Figure VII give a similar analysis of the data for the Day Schools and the Institutions in regard to the number of years the child has attended a school for hearing children.

TABLE 15

INCREASE IN EDUCATIONAL SURVEY TEST SCORES AS NUMBER OF YEARS SPENT IN A SCHOOL FOR HEARING CHILDREN INCREASES

Number of Years in a School for Hearing Children	Median Survey Test Score		Number of Cases	
	Day Schools	Institutions	Day Schools	Institutions
8 or more	54	63	8	9
6 or 7	53	48	27	8
4 or 5	52	39	28	9
2 or 3	35	28	33	15
0 or 1	27	19	215	1429

Again, there seems to be little difference in the slope of the curves for the two types of school. Both rise very rapidly for each additional two years that a school for hearing children has been attended. In the Day Schools there seems to be little difference in Educational Survey Test score after the children have been in a school for hearing children for four or five years, whereas among the Institutional children there is a rapid and steady increase until eight or more years in the school for hearing pupils has been reached. These curves, of course, represent

FIGURE VII. INCREASE IN SURVEY SCORE FOR EACH TWO YEARS SPENT IN A
SCHOOL FOR HEARING PUPILS

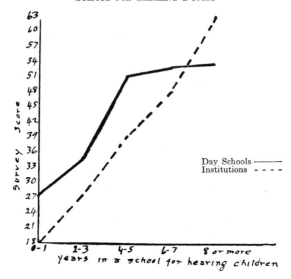

the influence of age of becoming deaf and probably degree of
residual hearing, as well as other factors which make for educational success such as the teaching efficiency of the school.
The rapid and steady increase among the Institutional children
is most important.

Table 16 and Figure IX give the analysis of the Educational
Survey Test scores in relation to increases in degree of residual
hearing, for both the Day Schools and the Institutions. In Figure IX there appears a somewhat definite difference between the
slopes of the curves for the two types of school. There seems
to be no tendency for an increase in the degree of residual hearing
to aid the children in the Institutions in gaining a higher score
on the Educational Survey Test. The 79 children with 60 per
cent or more of residual hearing do very little better in the
Educational Survey Test. Apparently, this factor of residual
hearing is unimportant in the education of children in the Institution. Unless some selective factor causes the children with a
greater degree of hearing to be younger, or more backward, than
the other children it seems fair to draw the conclusion that the
Institutions make practically no use of this aspect of the child's
equipment.

FIGURE VIII. INCREASE IN SURVEY SCORE FOR GIVEN AGES OF BECOMING DEAF

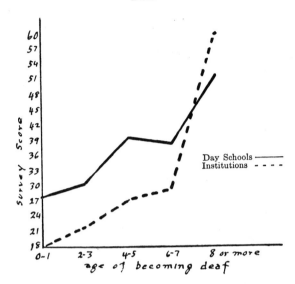

In the Day Schools considerable increase in the Educational Survey Test score is shown for those children who have 37 to 60 per cent of residual hearing, and a very definite increase in Educational Survey Test score is found for those children who have more than 60 per cent residual hearing. Apparently, the Day Schools take more advantage of the residual hearing of

TABLE 16

INCREASE OF EDUCATIONAL SURVEY TEST SCORE AS DEGREE OF RESIDUAL HEARING INCREASES

Degree of Hearing	Median of Survey Test Score		Number of Cases	
	Day Schools	Institutions	Day Schools	Institutions
61 and over	50	21	54	79
49 to 60	36	19	47	95
37 to 48	36	19	41	178
25 to 36	25	21	69	518
13 to 24	29	19	66	353
0 to 12	25	17	34	247

FIGURE IX. MEAN SURVEY SCORES FOR GIVEN DEGREES OF
RESIDUAL HEARING

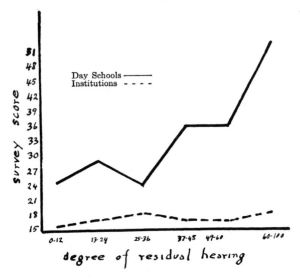

their children than do the Institutions in teaching the children under their care.

Figures VII, VIII, and IX suggest a study of the difference in Educational Survey Test score that would result if only those children in the Day School who had not been to a school for hearing children and who had become deaf before the age of two years were selected from the entire group and compared with the rest of the children in the Day Schools. Since the average Educational Survey Test score in the Institution is weighted much more heavily than the Day School score with the scores of children who were always deaf and have never attended a school for hearing pupils, the question arises as to what effect the variables we have just been considering have on educational achievement. The next chapter will discuss this problem.

CHAPTER VIII

DAY SCHOOL AND INSTITUTIONAL GROUPS MATCHED FOR FOUR VARIABLES

So far in this study it has been shown that the Day Schools are significantly superior to the Institutions in the educational achievement of their pupils, not only when all the children in both groups are measured, but also when the factor of intelligence is rendered constant by the process of selecting only those pupils from the Institutions who were equal in age and mental rating with those in the Day Schools. This method of attack brought to light significant positive differences in favor of the Day Schools in the following variables:

1. Maximum degree of hearing.
2. Years spent in a school for hearing children.
3. Age of becoming deaf.
4. Educational Survey Test score.

There were significant differences in favor of the Institutions in two variables:

1. Age of starting to school.
2. Years spent in a school for the deaf.

The fact that the mean age of starting Institutional pupils to school is greater than the mean age of starting Day School pupils to school would presumably give the Day School pupils an advantage educationally, provided that the age of leaving school was the same. The favorable effect on the Educational Survey Test scores of the pupils' having been longer in a deaf school, may be counterbalanced by the longer period of time the Day School pupils have spent in a school for hearing children. So far few data have been obtained on this problem and no one has made a study of the relative value of a certain period of time in a school for the deaf compared with the same period in a school for hearing children.

The effect of a greater average degree of hearing and of a later age of becoming deaf have been shown in previous studies and reports by Fusfeld, Pintner, and Reamer to be in the direction of a higher educational score. Thus the selection which the Day Schools exercise upon deaf children is almost entirely toward making easier the task of teaching the deaf children. Or stated in another way, the Day School should be able to achieve more educational advancement per unit of time and teaching ability than the Institutions can achieve.

In order to determine just which type of school for the deaf is producing the best results it will be necessary to make a still more careful comparison of the pupil populations.

How many of the factors which bear on educational achievement can be made constant in the two types of schools? How many should be made constant? No answer was available to the second of these questions, but there was some information which suggested the possibility of an answer to the first question. As previously stated, Pintner in his analysis of the survey by the National Research Council, found a rapid rise in the Educational Survey Test score for each year that children had had hearing after the age of four or five. Reamer, in her study, found the same tendency, except that she reports the critical age as five or six. It seemed desirable, then, to render constant this factor of age of becoming deaf. A study of the distributions of age of becoming deaf for the two groups shows a large number of pupils in both types of schools who were reported as deaf before the age of one year. Table 17 gives these distributions. It is probable that the children reported as becoming deaf before one year of age are congenital cases, but there is no accurate way of determining this fact. If this were true it may have some effect on the intelligence of the pupils, and consequently on the Educational Survey Test score. In order to render unimportant the influence of differences between the groups in this factor, as well as to make chronological age and mental ability constant, only the pupils already matched for these traits were used in the study about to be described. It is readily seen from Table 17 that the maximum number of cases having the common trait of being reported deaf before the age of one year is 143. For two reasons it was desirable to render constant the factor of years spent in a school for hearing children. The first was that, in the previous analysis, the factors of years spent in a school for the deaf and years spent in a school for hearing children were separate variables so far as tabulation was concerned, but the influence of one upon the other was very great—especially in the Day School group, the correlation in this group between these two variables being —.69 ± .02. In the evaluation of results of this analysis the Day School pupils were found to have spent much more

TABLE 17

Percentage of Day School Pupils and of the 1,470 Institutional Pupils Who Became Deaf at Each Age Level from 0 to 14

Age of Becoming Deaf	Day Schools		Institutions	
	Number	Per Cent	Number	Per Cent
14	1	0	1	0
13	0	0	0	0
12	3	1	2	0
11	1	0	0	0
10	4	1	3	.25
9	7	2	3	.25
8	5	2	7	.5
7	8	2	17	1
6	12	4	19	1
5	20	6	30	2
4	26	8	40	3
3	15	5	71	5
2	33	11	153	10
1	33	11	227	15
0–0.9	143	46	897	61
Total	311	99.0	1,470	99.0

time in schools for hearing children and the Institutional children a much longer time in schools for the deaf. The possibility of interpreting these two results in terms of influence on educational achievement was small.

The second reason will be referred to again. It was found that the most important variable in Day Schools, after degree of mental ability, for predicting the Educational Survey Test score was years spent in schools for hearing children. It will be seen from the distributions in Table 18 that there are 203 cases in the Day Schools which might be matched for years spent in a school for hearing children with cases in the Institutions. An attempt was made, therefore, to match Day School cases with Institutional cases who were similar in the following traits:

1. Chronological age.
2. P. N. L. score.
3. Age of becoming deaf reported as less than one year.
4. Less than one year spent in a school for hearing children.

TABLE 18

PERCENTAGE FOR EACH YEAR OF ATTENDANCE IN A SCHOOL FOR HEARING
PUPILS OF DAY SCHOOL AND INSTITUTIONAL CHILDREN

Years in School for Hearing Children	Day Schools		Institutions	
	Number	Per Cent	Number	Per Cent
11	1	0	0	0
10	1	0	1	0
9	3	1	1	0
8	3	1	7	1
7	11	4	3	0
6	16	5	5	0
5	13	4	6	1
4	15	5	3	0
3	13	4	5	0
2	21	7	10	1
1	11	4	36	2
0–0.9	203	65	1,393	95
Total	311	100	1,470	100

Eighty-three cases were found which could be so matched. Tables 19, 20, 21, and 22 give the distributions for both types of schools for the following variables which must now be analyzed: Educational Survey Test score, audiometer maximum, age of starting to school, and years spent in schools for the deaf. The differences between the means, the sigma of the differences between the means, and the chances in 100 that the differences are significant are found in Table 23. None of the differences are statistically significant, although there are 99 chances in 100 that the difference between the means of the Day Schools and the Institutions in regard to Educational Survey Test score is significant. The other data which have been presented make it seem likely that if a larger number of cases had been used the difference between the two groups would have become significant. Although this is not absolutely certain, as defined, it indicates that the probabilities are very high that the Day Schools secure better results from their teaching, even when the children taught are similar to the children taught in the Institutions in respect to chronological age, mental ability as measured by the Pintner Non-Language Test, age of deafness, and number of years spent in a school for hearing pupils.

TABLE 19

COMPARISON OF THE 83 MATCHED CASES IN REGARD TO
AGE OF STARTING SCHOOL

Age of Starting to School	Frequency	
	Day Schools	Institutions
12	1	1
11	1	3
10	2	2
9	5	4
8	8	12
7	17	20
6	26	21
5	17	14
4–4.9	6	6
Total	83	83
Mean	7.0 years	7.2 years
S. D.	1.5	1.7

Table 24 shows the tendency of the means of the Educational Survey Test scores in the Day Schools and Institutions to approach one another as groups are compared which are more and more comparable, in respect to the many factors which seem to influence the educational achievement of the deaf. When the Day School pupils' educational achievement is compared with that of children in the Institutions of the same age and mental ability the difference between the two types of schools is reduced by 2 points, or about 16 per cent. When those children are compared who in addition to being of equal age and mental ability, became deaf before the age of one and never attended a school for hearing children the difference between the Institutions and the Day Schools in educational achievement is reduced 5.2 points, or 50 per cent.

When groups of pupils from the Day Schools and the Institutions who had not attended a school for hearing children and who became deaf before one year of age and who were equal in chronological age and P. N. L. scores are compared, the dif-

TABLE 20

COMPARISON OF THE 83 MATCHED CASES IN REGARD TO PINTNER EDUCATIONAL SURVEY TEST SCORE

Survey Test Score	Frequency	
	Day Schools	Institutions
84	..	1
78	1	0
72	2	2
66	3	0
60	2	0
54	4	2
48	3	4
42	7	6
36	5	7
30	12	5
24	7	8
18	12	16
12	8	12
6	11	12
0–5.9	6	8
Total	83	83
Mean	30.5	25.6
S. D.	19.8	17.4

ference in residual hearing between the Day School and the Institution disappears. Table 23 also shows this fact.

It is interesting to note that the mean residual hearing for the 83 cases, in both Day Schools and Institutions, is less than the mean of all the cases. Those children who become deaf before the age of one never have as much residual hearing as other children. Table 25 shows that the variability of these children in residual hearing is less than for all deaf children.

The method of selection that was used for this analysis seems to have rendered the two groups of pupils equal, or almost equal, in degree of hearing. Instead of the critical ratio (i.e., the ratio of a difference to the sigma of the difference) of 5.6 between the 311 Day School cases and the 311 Institutional cases there is a ratio of .18. This means that there are only 58 chances out of 100 that the true difference will be greater than zero. This

TABLE 21

COMPARISON OF THE 83 MATCHED CASES IN REGARD TO
MAXIMUM RESIDUAL HEARING

Audiometer Maximum	Frequency	
	Day Schools	Institutions
84	1	0
78	0	1
72	0	0
66	0	0
60	1	0
54	2	0
48	3	3
42	4	5
36	4	11
30	17	13
24	13	16
18	20	14
12	11	10
6	4	7
0–5.9	3	3
Total	83	83
Mean	27.6	27.3
S. D.	14.0	13.1

is little more than a chance difference. In regard to the other two variables studied, i.e., number of years spent in a school for the deaf and the age of starting to school, there are only small differences between the groups. There are 84 chances out of 100 that the children in the Institutions have had a shorter period of time in the school for the deaf than the Day School children. This is far from being sufficient proof for a statement that the Institutions keep the children longer in school than do the Day Schools. It would probably be nearer the truth to say that there is no difference between the groups in this variable. The same is true of the age of starting to school. The ratio of 1.08 gives 86 chances out of 100 of the true difference being greater than zero. Conversely, there are 14 chances out of 100, or 1 in 7, that the true difference would indicate that the children in Institutions who qualify for the groups we are studying, start to school as early as, or earlier than, children in the Day Schools.

TABLE 22

COMPARISONS OF THE 83 MATCHED CASES IN REGARD TO
YEARS SPENT IN SCHOOLS FOR DEAF

Years Spent in Schools for Deaf	Frequency	
	Day Schools	Institutions
13	0	1
12	4	3
11	2	6
10	13	7
9	13	12
8	8	8
7	14	11
6	12	15
5	11	9
4	3	8
3	3	1
2	..	1
1–1.9	..	1
Total	83	83
Mean	8.0 years	7.8 years
S. D.	2.2	2.5

Figures X and XI show the closeness of the equating of the 83 children from the Institution with the 83 children from the Day Schools in chronological age and Pintner Non-Language Test. All the data show that the two groups are practically identical in age and mental ability as measured by the Pintner Non-Language Test.

Besides the light that this analysis throws on the quality of teaching in two types of schools as measured by the Pintner Educational Survey Test, it is of considerable interest in showing

FIGURE X. CLOSENESS OF MATCHING IN CHRONOLOGICAL AGE FOR 83
MATCHED PAIRS.

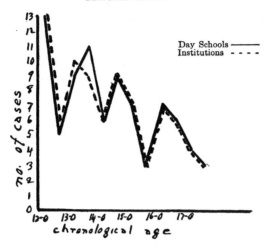

FIGURE XI. CLOSENESS OF MATCHING IN MENTAL ABILITY FOR 83
MATCHED CASES

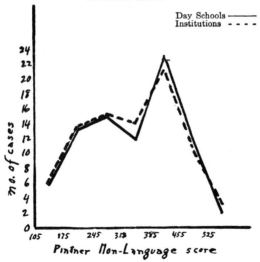

what effect on the other variables is produced by selecting only
those children who have been deaf since one year of age and
who have not been to a school for hearing pupils. Of particular
interest is the effect such a selection has on the other variables

TABLE 23

SIGNIFICANCE OF DIFFERENCES BETWEEN THE 83 CASES IN THE DAY SCHOOLS
MATCHED WITH THE 83 CASES FROM THE INSTITUTIONS FOR C. A.,
P. N. L. SCORE, YEARS IN SCHOOLS FOR HEARING CHILDREN AND
AGE OF BECOMING DEAF

Variable	Difference	S. D.Diff.	$\dfrac{\text{Diff.}}{\text{S. D.Diff.}}$	Chances in 100 That Difference Is Significant
Survey Test Score	4.7	2.13	2.22	99
Audiometer Maximum	.36	1.99	.18	58
Years in Schools for Deaf .	.24	.25	.96	84
Age of Starting to School ...	.25	.23	1.08	86

within the Day School group. Table 25 has been prepared, not only to show the means for each of the four groups, i.e., (1) the Day School group of 311 cases, (2) the Day School group of 83 cases, (3) the Institutional group of 311 cases, (4) the Institutional group of 83 cases, but also the influence of this selection on the variability of the groups as shown by their standard deviations.

The fact that the 83 cases from the Day Schools have a mean amount of residual hearing which is practically the same as the 83 cases from the Institutions has already been discussed.

The mean of 27.3 for the Institutional group of 83 cases is only 1.8 points lower than the mean of 29.10 for the total Institutional group of 311 cases and only 1.08 points lower than the mean of the whole Institutional group of 1,470 cases. This small difference is probably explained by the fact that out of the 1,470 Institutional cases 897 cases were reported as being deaf before one year of age, and 380 other cases were reported as deaf before three years of age. That is, 61 per cent would be included in the group we are studying and 87 per cent were reported as being deaf before they had attained the age of three years. On the other hand, in the Day School group of 311 cases 46 per cent were found to have been deaf at birth, or before one year of age, and 67 per cent before three years of age. If, as seems likely, in the Day Schools there is a tendency for those who became deaf later in life to have a greater degree of residual hearing, the large

TABLE 24

Differences Between the Day Schools and the Institutions in Regard
to Educational Survey Test Score and Audiometer Maximum
Score for Three Different Comparisons

Groups Compared	Mean Score				Difference	
	Day Schools		Institutions			
	Survey Test Score	Audiometer Maximum	Survey Test Score	Audiometer Maximum	Survey Test Score	Audiometer Maximum
311 Day School Cases with 1,470 Institutional Cases	35.4	37.8	23.3	28.4	12.1	7.0
311 Day School Cases with 311 Institutional Cases When Cases Are Equated for C. A. and P. N. L.	35.4	37.8	25.3	29.1	10.1	6.3
83 Day School Cases with 83 Institutional Cases When Cases Are Equated for C. A., P. N. L., Years in Schools for Hearing Children, and Age of Becoming Deaf	30.5	27.6	25.6	27.3	4.9	.3

TABLE 25

Means and Sigmas in Six Variables for Four of the Groups Studied

Variable	Means				Sigmas			
	Day Schools		Institutions		Day Schools		Institutions	
	311 Cases	83 Cases	311 Cases	83 Cases	311 Cases	83 Cases	311 Cases	83 Cases
C. A.	14–6.5	14–5.1	14–6.3	14–4.9	19.09	19.8	19.12	20.0
P. N. L. Score	340.9	344.2	341.49	343.0	99.57	108.85	99.34	110.25
Survey Test Score	35.40	30.5	25.32	25.6	22.05	19.8	17.02	17.04
Audiometer Maximum .	37.80	27.6	29.10	27.3	21.42	14.0	16.50	13.1
Number of Years in Schools for Deaf	6.29	7.6	7.26	7.8	3.02	2.2	2.43	2.5
Age of Starting to School	7.19	7.0	7.69	7.2	1.77	1.5	1.796	1.7

FIGURE XII.   DAY SCHOOLS.   MEAN DEGREES OF RESIDUAL HEARING FOR
GIVEN AGES OF BECOMING DEAF

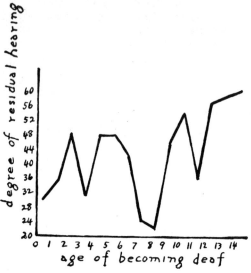

FIGURE XIII.   INSTITUTIONS.   MEAN DEGREES OF RESIDUAL HEARING FOR
GIVEN AGES OF BECOMING DEAF

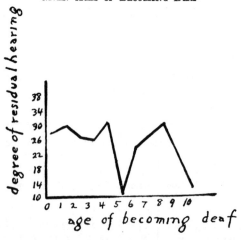

difference in one case and the much smaller difference in the
other case may be explained by these percentages. Figure
XII shows the tendency of the degree of residual hearing to
increase as the age of becoming deaf increases. The figure is

based on the data of the 311 Day School cases. (The median residual hearing for each age of becoming deaf is used.) The number of cases after the age of five is relatively small, and the medians are consequently very unreliable. However, a distinct tendency toward increase in degree of hearing with increase in age of becoming deaf is visible, although the curve is very uneven. Figure XIII shows the data for the group of 311 Institutional cases. Here there is no well-marked tendency up or down but the numbers for each age, except for the first two or three, are much too small to give a reliable trend. Hence, with the trend being slightly upward in the Day School group and being practically horizontal in the Institutional group, and with the medians for both groups at zero age of deafness nearly equal, the great decrease in the 83 Day School cases is accounted for, although the problem as to why there is an upward trend in one case and no such trend in the other is not solved.

Not only are the means for the degree of residual hearing in both groups lower than was previously found, but the variability has been greatly restricted. In the 311 Day School cases the standard deviation was 21.42. In the 83 Day School cases this has been lowered to 14.0—a difference of 7.42 points. In the Institutional group the decrease is 3.49 points. The two sigmas for the two 83 case groups are almost alike, i.e., 14.0 for the Day Schools and 13.1 for the Institutions.

An examination of the means and sigmas of the Pintner Non-Language Test shows an interesting feature. Both C. A.'s of the 83 groups are slightly lower than the C. A.'s of the 311 groups whereas both Non-Language means are slightly above the Non-Language means of the 311 group. In terms of intelligence quotient, the process of picking only those who became deaf before the age of one year and who had not been to a school for hearing children, seems to have selected those with slightly greater intelligence quotients. At the same time there is a marked increase in the variability of the P.N.L. Test for these groups over either the 311 cases from Day Schools or the 311 cases from Institutions. The variability is not so great, however, as for the whole group of Institutional cases, the sigma for the whole group being 119.00. This increase of spread in mental ability is not accompanied by a similar increase in chronological age. The sigmas for all groups are practically the same.

The 83 Institutional cases have practically the same mean Educational Survey Test score as the group of 311 cases. The sigma remained the same also. Apparently, the two groups are alike in this variable. This is not true of the 83 Day School cases and the larger group of 311. There is a decrease of 4.9 points in the mean of the more selected group and a decrease of 2.25 in the standard deviation. This sigma of 19.8 is still 2.4 points above the sigma of the Institutional group. The teaching and other factors which we have not studied make the Day School children more variable in educational achievement even when chronological age, mental ability, age of becoming deaf, and years in a school for hearing children are kept constant and the degree of hearing and time spent in school of the two groups are practically the same.

One other factor has been studied which might be thought to influence the scores on the educational test. This factor is the method of teaching. If the oral method is superior to the other methods the Day Schools might be gaining some of their superiority from this cause, for, although most schools, both Day Schools and Institutions, now use the oral method, the Day Schools early claimed the method as a distinctive feature of their system of education. Pintner's report, however, shows the apparent lack of influence on the educational score of the method of teaching. He concludes "that no one method is superior to the others with reference to the educational achievement of the pupils, when we take into consideration their basic intelligence." [23]

The data on which this study is based are not of such nature as to allow a study of teaching efficiency in the two types of schools. Such a study would be extremely important in determining whether or not this factor is responsible for the inferior educational product (as measured by the Pintner Educational Survey Test) found in the average Institution for the deaf, compared with that found in the average Day School for the deaf.

Of the various factors which have been considered as important influences on the educational achievement of the child, that of teacher efficiency has not been considered in this study. Consequently there is no proof that this factor is the one which is responsible for the superior educational knowledge of the Day

Schools. Since the other factors—chronological age, mental ability, age of becoming deaf, degree of residual hearing, and years spent in school have been made constant, and since the method of teaching is reported to have no influence when these factors are taken into consideration, and since there yet remains a significant difference in educational achievement—99 chances out of 100 that it is significant—it seems reasonable to suppose that this factor of teacher efficiency may be responsible for some of the difference.

CHAPTER IX

RELATIONSHIPS EXISTING BETWEEN THE VARIABLES

In the preceding chapter our attention was focused primarily on the differences between the Day Schools and the Institutions, with a view to finding out the real difference in educational achievement between the pupils of these two kinds of schools. In this chapter attention will be directed primarily toward the relationships which exist between the variables which are included in this study. The most valuable technique for this purpose is that of correlation. This method will therefore be employed. The foregoing discussion has shown the wide differences between the variables in the two types of schools. It naturally follows that these groups should be treated separately in any analysis which has as its object the determination of the relationships existing between the variables. If these groups were thrown together, conclusions based on the results would be of little value to either type of school, and would give information about a mathematical whole which, in reality, was not a homogeneous entity.

Moreover, there are certain differences between the selected group of 311 Institutional cases and the whole group of Institutional children which might affect the results detrimentally; hence these two groups have been treated as separate units in the following analysis. We have, then, three distinct groups, each of which must be studied with a view to finding out the relationships of the various traits for which we have measurements.

For purposes of clarity a list of the traits for which numerical measurements are available is presented. The same traits were measured in each of the three groups. As was indicated at the beginning of this report, measurements are available for all the variables for each child included in each of the groups. This fact should be borne in mind when the results are evaluated, for it makes all the intercorrelations within a group comparable.

1. Chronological age (in years and months).
2. Pintner Non-Language Test score.
3. Pintner Rapid Survey Test score.
4. Audiometer left.
5. Audiometer right.
6. Audiometer maximum.
7. Years in school for the deaf.
8. Years in school for the hearing.
9. Age of starting to school.
10. Age at which deafness occurred.

A discussion of the reliability of the measures used is in order before the interrelationships of the variables are analyzed. Most of the variables do not lend themselves readily to the determination of a reliability coefficient. Five of the variables, (1) chronological age, (2) years in a school for deaf children, (3) years in a school for normal hearing children, (4) age of starting to school, and (5) age at which deafness occurred, are matters of fact which were reported on the questionnaire. No method was used to check the reliability of this information. A careful attempt was made by the author to reduce the number of errors in this information to a minimum. For example, if a child attended school steadily from the time of starting until the questionnaire was filled out, the sum of years spent in a school for the deaf plus the years spent in a school for the hearing, plus the age of starting to school must equal the chronological age. In the selection of cases to be used in this study all cases were discarded where the above condition did not hold true. That is, if the sum of the age of starting to school and the years spent in the two types of schools did not come within a year of the chronological age, the case was not used. This procedure excluded all those pupils who had missed a number of years in their school careers, thus removing another possible source of variation in the results.

There was no possible way of determining the accuracy of the report on age at which deafness occurred. Since this information came from the parents in the large majority of cases, and, since in many cases no written medical statement was available, the probabilities are that the ages given are not absolutely accurate. Inasmuch as deafness is frequently not noticed for a few months after the birth of the child, there is likely to be a constant error toward reporting the age of becoming deaf as greater than the true figure. This would make a difference in the means of this variable, but would not be so likely to affect the variability or the coefficients of correlation.

For the audiometer no accurate index of reliability is available. No data were found which give the coefficient of correlation between a first and a second test of residual hearing by means of the 3A audiometer. This information should be obtained before a thorough knowledge of the usefulness of the audiometer can be ascertained. The data used in this study yield a rough measure of reliability in that audiometer readings of both left and right ears were taken. There seems to be no reason to suppose that the hearing of both ears should be the same among deaf children. If it could be assumed that the degree of residual hearing in each ear is the same, then the correlation between the hearing of the right ear with the hearing of the left ear would give a reliability coefficient. But this probably cannot be assumed. It would seem, however, that the reliability coefficient would be at least as great as this coefficient, for the relationship would be lowered, not only by unreliability of the audiometer readings, but by discrepancies in the real amounts of hearing in the two ears.

On the other hand, since the two ears were tested one after the other on the same day there may have been an unconscious tendency to bring the ratings of the two ears together.

In the group of 311 Day School cases, the Pearson product-moment coefficient of correlation between the degree of hearing in the right ear and that in the left is .735 ± .02. In the Institutional group of 311 cases the coefficient is .699 ± .02. Each of these coefficients is fairly high. Of course, if the reliability were really no higher than this, the audiometer scores could not be used profitably with individual cases. It would seem that the true reliability of this instrument is at least as great as that indicated by the above coefficients.

There is only one form of the Pintner Non-Language Test and one of the Pintner Educational Survey Test. Reliability coefficients based on giving equivalent forms of the test are therefore impossible. No reliability coefficients have been computed by correlating one half of the tests against the other and correcting the coefficient by the Spearman Brown formula. However, certain indications of the reliability of these tests are available. Pintner [25] reports that for a group of 201 hearing pupils in grades 4, 5, and 6 the correlation between a first attempt of the Pintner Non-Language Test and a second attempt two days later is .79 ± .017. The correlation was based on raw scores.

An indication of the reliability of the Non-Language Test and the Educational Survey Tests is reported by Pintner [24] for deaf children. In one school for the deaf 26 children were given the Non-Language Test and the Educational Survey Test in 1919 and again in 1923. The correlation between the scores of the two trials on the Non-Language Test was .72 ± .06,* that for the Educational Survey Test was .70 ± .06. When the index is used instead of crude scores, the correlation coefficient increases to .80 ± .04 for each test.

In another deaf school 91 pupils took the two tests twice—once in 1919 and once in 1922. The correlation between the mental indices for this group was .75 ± .03. The correlation between the educational indices was .77 ± .03. The use of indices introduces an element of spurious correlation, but the correlations based on crude scores are only slightly lower than those based upon indices. Presumably, the amount of spurious correlation is relatively small.

The reliability of these two tests is not high when compared with the best of modern tests for hearing children. However, for groups of children correlations between .70 and .80 give sufficiently reliable results for practical purposes. For individuals, predictions based on such coefficients would be highly unreliable, as indicated by the coefficient of alienation [20]. For a correlation of .80—the highest that has been reported for reliability of these tests the coefficient of alienation is .60. This may be roughly interpreted as being only two-fifths better than chance.

A discussion of the interrelationships of the variables is now in order. Table 26 gives all the intercorrelations for the ten variables used for the Day School group of 311 children.

Our most important problem is to find out the relation that each of these variables bears to educational achievement as measured by the Pintner Educational Survey Test. As has been

* The P.E.'s have been calculated by the writer. They are not given in the report by Pintner.

TABLE 26

PEARSON PRODUCT-MOMENT INTERCORRELATION COEFFICIENTS BETWEEN THE VARIABLES STUDIED IN THE DAY SCHOOLS

	C. A.	P. N. L. Score	Survey Test Score	Audiometer Left	Audiometer Right	Audiometer Maximum	Years in Schools for Deaf	Years in Schools for Hearing	Age of Starting to School	Age of Becoming Deaf
C. A.		.33	.28	– .07	– .06	– .07	.41	.03	.15	.02
P. N. L. Score			.53	– .04	– .02	– .05	.38	– .01	– .32	– .02
Survey Test Score ...				.25	.29	.28	.01	.42	– .32	.24
Audiometer Left					.74	.92	– .40	.49	– .07	.18
Audiometer Right						.87	– .35	.47	– .09	.13
Audiometer Maximum							– .40	.50	– .08	.20
Years in Schools for Deaf								– .69	– .27	– .45
Years in Schools for Hearing									– .20	.53
Age of Starting to School										.01
Age of Becoming Deaf										

The P.E.'s of the correlation coefficients in this table may be readily determined from the table in Appendix II.

frequently found in the past, when normal hearing children are used as subjects the mental ability of the children has the greatest degree of relationship with educational standing. Table 26 shows the Pearson r to be .53 ± .03 between these two traits. The next highest coefficient is between the Educational Survey Test score and the number of years spent in a school for hearing pupils. This correlation is .42 ± .03. This relationship is at first very surprising. But more surprising yet is the coefficient between the Educational Survey Test score and number of years spent in a school for the deaf. This coefficient is only .01 ± .04. So far as this group of Day School pupils is concerned, there is apparently only a chance relationship between the number of years spent in a school for the deaf and the score received on the Educational Survey Test. In a later section of this chapter it will be shown that this r of .01 does not express the true relationship existing between educational achievement and number of years spent in a school for deaf children. Another important coefficient is the negative one of —.32 ± .03 between the Educational Survey Test score and the age of starting to school. There is a marked tendency for those who start to school early to receive the highest scores on the Educational Survey Test. Other things being equal, this is as one would expect. The Pearson r between the Educational Survey Test score and the age at which deafness occurred is marked but not high, i.e., .2377 ± .04. Somewhat similar coefficients exist between the Educational Survey Test scores and the various audiometer scores:

Survey Test Score and Audiometer Left .... .25 ± .04
Survey Test Score and Audiometer Right .... .29 ± .04
Survey Test Score and Audiometer Maximum .... .28 ± .04

The third highest coefficient between the Educational Survey Test scores and the other variables is that of .3263 ± .03 with chronological age. Apparently, chronological age is a relatively important factor in the educational advancement of these children.

Table 26 shows that in the Day School group none of the variables correlate very highly with educational achievement as measured by the Educational Survey Test. If it is assumed that all the correlation coefficients are linear (this assumption is shown to be untrue for several of the relationships), the multiple correlation coefficient will yield a prediction of the extent to which a combination of all the variables will foretell educational achievement. This coefficient is .7128. Mental ability is the most important of the variables for predicting educational success. Number of years spent in a school for hearing pupils is next and not much less important; then chronological age comes next but adds comparatively little as compared with the first two variables. Table 27 gives the Beta weights found during the process of calculating the multiple correlation coefficient.

TABLE 27

BETA WEIGHTS FOR THE VARIABLES USED TO PREDICT EDUCATIONAL ACHIEVEMENT AMONG DAY SCHOOL PUPILS

P. N. L. Score	.4400
Years in Schools for Hearing	.3184
C. A.	.1404
Audiometer Maximum	.1186
Age of Starting to School	−.1089
Age of Becoming Deaf	.0861
Years in Schools for Deaf	.0710

The value of the multiple correlation technique is questionable because the Pearson product-moment coefficient does not give the full amount of the relationships between some of these variables.* However, Table 27 gives an indication of the importance of each of these variables for the purpose of predicting scores on the Educational Survey Test.

Table 28 gives the Pearson r's for the intercorrelations in the Institutional group of 311 cases. There is a striking difference between these correlations and the corresponding correlations for the Day School group. The causes which operated to produce the great differences which were found to exist between these two groups of deaf children by the methods used in earlier chapters apparently exert such an influence that many of the correlation coefficients are also widely different.

The first great difference is that for correlation between chronological age and Educational Survey Test score, the coefficients being 28 for the Day Schools and 43 for the Institutions. From Table 29 it is seen that the degree of relationship for the 1,159 remaining Institutional cases is almost identical with that

* See page 67.

TABLE 28

PEARSON PRODUCT-MOMENT INTERCORRELATION COEFFICIENTS BETWEEN THE VARIABLES STUDIED IN THE GROUP OF 311 INSTITUTIONAL CHILDREN

	C. A.	P. N. L. Score	Survey Test Score	Audi-ometer Maximum	Years in Schools for Deaf	Years in Schools for Hearing	Age of Starting to School	Age of Becoming Deaf
C. A.		.33	.43	− .08	.56	− .03	.16	.05
P. N. L. Score			.64	− .01	.40	.01	− .25	.09
Survey Test Score				− .03	.40	.15	− .23	.21
Audiometer Maximum					− .12	.14	.06	− .01
Years in Schools for Deaf ...						− .38	− .61	− .27
Years in Schools for Hearing							− .02	.44
Age of Starting to School ...								.18
Age of Becoming Deaf								

The P. E.'s for the correlation coefficients in this table may be readily determined from the table in Appendix II. Only the audiometer maximum scores were used in correlations with the other variables in this group.

TABLE 29

SELECTED INTERCORRELATIONS BASED ON 1,159 INSTITUTIONAL CASES

	C. A.	P. N. L. Score	Survey Test Score	Audiometer Maximum	Years in Schools for Deaf	Years in Schools for Hearing	Age of Starting to School	Age of Becoming Deaf
C. A.		.32	.44		.56			
P. N. L. Score			.67		.46		−.36	
Survey Test Score				.05	.47	.28		.23
Audiometer Maximum								.04
Years in Schools for Deaf								
Years in Schools for Hearing							−.69	
Age of Starting to School								
Age of Becoming Deaf								

The P. E.'s for the correlation coefficients in this table may be readily determined from the table in Appendix II.

gained when the 311 cases were used. The difference is only .01. Thus, the degree of association between chronological age and educational achievement as measured by the Educational Survey Test is markedly greater among children attending Institutions than among children attending Day Schools. This difference cannot be accounted for by differences in variability of the Day School group and the Institutional group. From Tables 6, 7, and 8 it is seen that the sigmas for chronological age in the three groups are the same, and that the sigmas for the Educational Survey Test scores in the Day School is 22 as compared with 17 for each Institutional group. Other things being equal, this would increase the r for the Day School; but the reverse is true.

The next large difference is in correlations between chronological age and years spent in a school for the deaf, the coefficients being .41 for the Day School and .56 for both groups from the Institutions. Here again there is a greater degree of relationship between the two variables in the Institutional group than in the Day School group.

The Non-Language Test scores have a greater association with educational achievement in the Institutions than in the Day Schools, the difference being that indicated by a rise in the coefficient from .53 in the Day School to .64 in the Institutional group of 311 cases and to .675 in the 1,159 remaining Institutional cases.

The r's between the Non-Language Test scores and the years in a school for the deaf show a slight increase in size in favor of the Institutions, .38 for the Day Schools, .40 for the 311 Institutional cases, and .46 for the 1,159 Institutional cases.

The substantial but not very large negative correlation between the age of starting to school and the score on the Non-Language Test is very interesting. It would seem that among deaf children, at any rate, the age of starting to school has a definite relationship to the degree of intelligence as measured by the Pintner Non-Language Test. In other words, the more intelligent children have a tendency to start to school earlier than the less intelligent. However, there is no well-marked difference between the Day Schools and the Institutions in this respect. In the Day Schools, the coefficient of correlation is —.32; in the 311 Institutional cases, it is —.25; and in the 1,159 Institutional group it is —.36.

A very important difference is found between the relationship of the Pintner Educational Survey Test score and the maximum degree of hearing for the Day Schools and the Institutions. The correlation for the Day Schools is .28, which is very substantial but low. On the other hand, the correlation in the Institutional group of 311 cases is —.03 and in the group of 1,159 cases it is .05. Neither of these can be considered as showing any relationship whatever. Apparently, then, what degree of hearing the Institutional children possess makes no difference so far as their educational achievement is concerned, whereas in the Day Schools the higher amounts of residual hearing have some influence on the scores obtained on the Pintner Educational Survey Test. It would be very valuable for practical school administration if a critical score could be determined above which the residual hearing of the child might be used. The data from this investigation are not sufficient for determining the score, although an approximation to such a score will be made later. Moreover, the problem is rendered more difficult because of the possible influence of other factors, such as intelligence, on the extent to which the degree of residual hearing may be utilized.

In the Day Schools the number of years spent in a school for the deaf has no relationship, as measured by the Pearson r, with the Educational Survey Test score, whereas the number of years spent in a school for hearing pupils has considerable relationship, the coefficient of correlation being .42. In the Institutions there is a tendency for the reverse to be true. The correlation between number of years spent in a school for the deaf and the score on the Educational Survey Test is .40 in the group of 311 cases and .47 in the group of 1,159 cases. The correlation between years spent in a school for hearing pupils and score on the Educational Survey Test is .15 for the group of 311 cases and .28 for the group of 1,159 cases.

Another marked difference in correlation is that between years spent in a school for the deaf and maximum audiometer score. In the Institutional group of 311 cases there is barely any relationship ($r = .12$). But in the Day Schools a negative correlation of .40 is found. Similarly, the correlation between years spent in a school for hearing children and maximum audiometer score is relatively high in Day Schools, .50, but for the Institutional group of 311 cases it is only .14.

This low correlation between the years spent in a school for the deaf or a school for hearing pupils, by the children in Institutions is probably due to the fact that a very small percentage of children in the Institutions possess sufficient residual hearing to profit by the instruction in a school for hearing children. On the other hand, the Day Schools contain a sufficient percentage of children with relatively great degrees of residual hearing to make it probable that they attended a school for hearing children a number of years somewhat proportionate to the degree of hearing possessed, and consequently attended a school for deaf children a shorter period.

There is no correlation between the age at which deafness occurred and the amount of residual hearing among Institutional children but in the Day Schools there is a correlation of .20. One can only speculate on the cause of this. The Day Schools may cater to children who have become deaf for relatively less serious reasons than those children who go to the Institutions. And among such children there may be a slight relationship between degree of deafness and age of becoming deaf, whereas in children who have an hereditary tendency toward deafness there may be no relationship at all.

There is an astonishing difference between Day Schools and Institutions in the correlations between years in schools for the deaf and age of starting to school. In the Day Schools the correlation is —.27 but in the Institutional group of 311 cases it is —.61 and in the Institutional group of 1,159 cases it is —.69. In the Institutions, then, the longer time a child has spent in a deaf school the younger he was when he entered school. In the Day School there is some relationship between the variables but it is not great.

In the Day Schools there is no relationship between age of deafness and age of starting to school, but in the Institutions there is a slight tendency for those who become deaf early in life to begin school early. This may be due to the desire of the parents to place such children as soon as possible in a more appropriate environment than the home can afford.

Scatter diagrams of the data were plotted to give a visual check of the linearity of the various relationships reported. Although most of the correlations are low, so that the trends were not as clearly marked as when the correlations are high, several of the trends appeared definitely curvilinear. Figure XIV shows the most extreme example. Another method of handling the data became necessary. The correlation ratio was used. Table 30 gives the variables with the two correlation ratios for each of the variables correlated with the Educational Survey Test score and also the Pearson product-moment r, in (1) the Day Schools, (2) the Institutional group of 311 cases, and (3) the Institutional group of 1,159 cases. Table 31 gives the value of N $(\eta^2 - r^2)$ for each of the correlation ratios obtained. In the form of Blakeman's short test for linearity reported by Garrett, [4, 16] N $(\eta^2 - r^2)$ must be less than 11.37 in order that linearity may be assumed. The short test is applicable to these data, for both η and r are small with the exception of the

TABLE 30

COMPARISON OF CORRELATION RATIOS AND PEARSON r'S IN THE DAY SCHOOLS AND INSTITUTIONS

Educational Survey Test Score and	η	η Day Schools	Institutions 311 Cases	Institutions 1,159 Cases	Pearson r Day Schools	Institutions 311 Cases	Institutions 1,159 Cases
C. A.	yx	.348	.460	.465			
	xy	.357	.475	.465	.284	.431	.441
P. N. L. Score	yx	.558	.712	.852			
	xy	.567	.662	.736	.535	.641	.675
Audiometer Maximum	yx	.365	.196	.148			
	xy	.369	.226	.160	.282	.027	.053
Years in Schools for Deaf .	yx	.395	.487	.494			
	xy	.279	.548	.614	.014	.396	.469
Years in Schools for Hearing	yx	.471	.259	.319			
	xy	.461	.519	.462	.416	.151	.283
Age of Starting to School .	yx	.384	.261	....			
	xy	.404	.349	....	$-.324$	$-.228$	....
Age of Becoming Deaf	yx	.291	.245	.274			
	xy	.294	.354	.344	.238	.208	.232

The Educational Survey Test score is the y variable in this table.

TABLE 31

VALUES OF N ($\eta^2 - r^2$) FOR EACH CORRELATION RATIO

Educational Survey Test Score		Day Schools		Institutions			
				311 Cases		˜ 1,159 Cases	
		η	$N (\eta^2 - r^2)$	η	$N (\eta^2 - r^2)$	η	$N (\eta^2 - r^2)$
C. A.	yx	.348	12.58	.460	8.04	.465	25.20
	xy	.357	14.55	.475	12.40	.465	25.20
P. N. L. Score	yx	.558	7.82	.712	29.88	.852	313.25
	xy	.567	10.97	.662	8.51	.736	99.76
Audiometer Maximum ...	yx	.365	16.70	.196	11.72	.148	22.13
	yx	.369	17.61	.226	15.66	.160	26.41
Years in Schools for Deaf .	yx	.395	48.46	.487	24.99	.494	27.93
	xy	.279	24.15	.548	44.62	.614	182.00
Years in Schools for Hearing	yx	.471	15.17	.259	13.77	.319	25.12
	xy	.461	12.27	.519	76.68	.462	154.56
Age of Starting to School .	yx	.384	13.21	.261	5.02	....	....
	xy	.404	18.11	.349	21.71	....	....
Age of Becoming Deaf ...	yx	.291	8.72	.245	5.21	.274	24.63
	xy	.294	9.27	.354	25.52	.344	74.77

relationships between the Educational Survey Test score and the Non-Language Test score.

All but four of the N ($\eta^2 - r^2$) values in the Day Schools are above 11.37. The only linear relationships in the Day Schools between the Educational Survey Test score and the other variables are between the Educational Survey Test score and the Non-Language Test score, and between the Educational Survey Test score and age of becoming deaf. The curvilinearity is very slight between the Educational Survey Test score and (1) chronological age, and (2) years spent in a school for hearing pupils. As shown in Figures XIV, XV, and XVI, there is a marked curvilinear relationship between the Educational Survey Test score and the number of years spent in a school for deaf children.

Among the 311 cases from the Institutions there is no relationship that has both regression trends linear. There is linearity of regression for predicting educational achievement from

FIGURE XIV. DAY SCHOOLS. REGRESSION TRENDS FOR SURVEY TEST AND
YEARS IN A DEAF SCHOOL

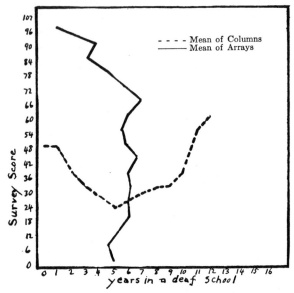

chronological age, score on Non-Language Test from Educational
Survey Test score, Educational Survey Test score from age of
starting to school, and Educational Survey Test score from age
of deafness. All the other regression trends are curvilinear.

Among the 1,159 Institutional cases there are no linear regression
trends.

Since so few of the regression lines are linear, it is impossible
to write equations predicting one variable from the other. For
the same reason the use of partial and multiple correlations
is impractical, especially in the Institutions where curvilinearity
is more frequent and more pronounced.

In the multiple correlation which has been reported for the
Day Schools, the variable of years spent in a school for the deaf
has not received its proper weight. Since the Blakeman short
test for linearity shows only slight curvilinearity between the
other variables in the Day Schools and the Educational Survey
Test score, it is probable that each of these has received approximately
its proper weight.

Figure XIV shows the one case of pronounced curvilinearity
in the Day School group. In predicting the score on the Educa-

FIGURE XV.   INSTITUTIONS (1,159).   REGRESSION TRENDS FOR SURVEY TEST
AND YEARS IN A DEAF SCHOOL

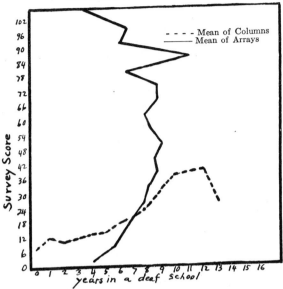

tional Survey Test from the number of years spent in a school
for the deaf (as shown by the broken line), until five years, there
is a negative relation between these two variables. That is, those
children who have been in a school for the deaf only one or two
years receive better scores on the Educational Survey Test than
those who have been in such a school five years. After five years
spent in a school for the deaf a positive relationship with educational achievement appears. A very sharp rise in score on the
Educational Survey Test takes place for the two or three years
after nine. The reason for the negative relationship in the first
five years is easily found, in that those children who become
deaf late in life or who have a relatively great degree of residual
hearing have attended schools for hearing children with marked
profit. Those who have been in a school for hearing children
longest have, other things being equal, been a shorter time in
a school for the deaf. Figure XVI shows that the same general
type of curve obtains in the Institutional group of 311 cases although the initial negative correlation is not so pronounced.
In the group of 1,159 cases (Figure XV) the initial negative
correlation has disappeared, but there is very little rise in Edu-

FIGURES XVI. INSTITUTIONS (311). REGRESSION TRENDS FOR SURVEY TEST
AND YEARS IN A DEAF SCHOOL

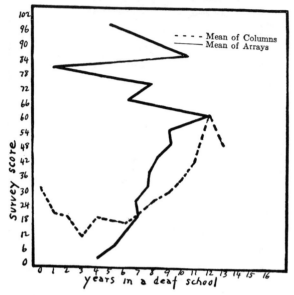

cational Survey Test score accompanying each year in the school
for the deaf until five or six years have been spent in the school
for the deaf. In each figure it is not until five or six years have
been spent in the school for the deaf that another year produces
a marked rise in educational score. This suggests that the Educational Survey Test does not test pupils in those respects in which
they show improvement during the first five or six years of
school. The mean age of starting to school is about seven, and it
takes about five or six years in a school for the deaf to enable
children to do the problems asked in the Educational Survey
Test. This would make children about twelve or thirteen before
they could obtain satisfactory scores on the test. Thus the decision of the National Research Council to test only those children
who were twelve years of age or older is justified.

Figures XVII, XVIII, and XIX show the regression trends
for the three groups under consideration, for the relationships
between scores on the Educational Survey Test and scores on
the Non-Language Test. Figure XVII, which gives the regression trends for the Day Schools, shows the small amount of
curvilinearity revealed by the Blakeman short test. In the group

FIGURE XVII. DAY SCHOOLS. REGRESSION TRENDS FOR SURVEY TEST AND
PINTNER NON-LANGUAGE TEST

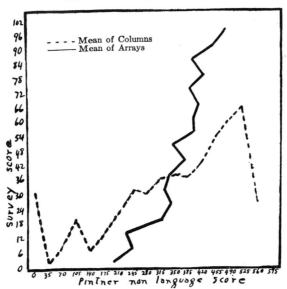

FIGURE XVIII. INSTITUTIONS (1,159). REGRESSION TRENDS FOR SURVEY
TEST AND PINTNER NON-LANGUAGE TESTS

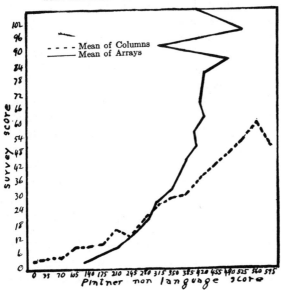

FIGURE XIX. INSTITUTIONS (311). REGRESSION TRENDS FOR SURVEY TEST
AND PINTNER NON-LANGUAGE TEST

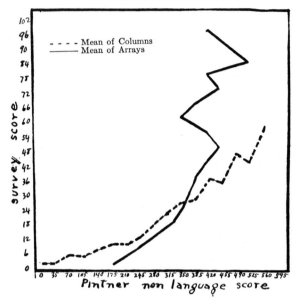

of 311 cases there is slightly more curvilinearity present, whereas in the large group of 1,159 cases the curvilinearity is marked in both trends. The general slope of the curves is the same for both groups of Institutional cases. For predicting the score on the Non-Language Test from the score on the Educational Survey Test the line giving the means of the arrays (i.e., the solid line) must be used. A small increase in score on Educational Survey Test at the lower end of the scale is accompanied by a large increase in score on the Non-Language Test. In other words, a slight gain in educational achievement among those who can barely do the Educational Survey Test requires a relatively large increase in the score indicating mental ability. As the test becomes easier for the children, relatively smaller gains in mental ability score accompany increases in the test score; increases in test score beyond 50 are accompanied by practically no increase in mental ability rating.

If the score on the Educational Survey Test is to be predicted from the Non-Language Test score (the broken line), the same general tendency is observable; that is, at the lower end of the

FIGURE XX. DAY SCHOOLS. REGRESSION TRENDS FOR SURVEY TEST AND AGE AT WHICH DEAFNESS OCCURRED

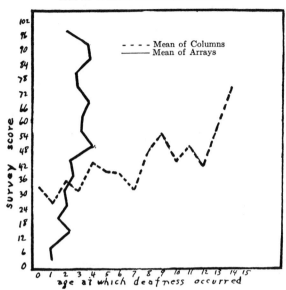

scale for Non-Language Test scores large gains in mental ability score are accompanied by very small gains in educational achievement. As the mental ability score increases, a given unit is accompanied by larger and larger gains in educational achievement. However, there is no definite flattening of the curve at the upper end.

Figures XX and XXI show the regression trends for the Day School group and the Institutional group of 1,159 cases for the relationship between score on Educational Survey Test and age at which deafness occurred. The Institutional group of 311 cases is not shown, since it almost exactly duplicates the group of 1,159 cases. In predicting the educational score from the age at which deafness occurred in the Institutional group, Figure XXI shows that each successive year at which deafness occurred, up to and including the fourth year, is accompanied by a slight increase in educational score. Previous reports have not emphasized this finding. There is no increase for the fifth, sixth, or seventh years. At the eighth year there is a marked increase in educational score. The score on the Educational Survey Test for each of the succeeding years is definitely above the level for

FIGURE XXI. INSTITUTIONS (1,159). REGRESSION TRENDS FOR SURVEY TEST
AND AGE AT WHICH DEAFNESS OCCURRED

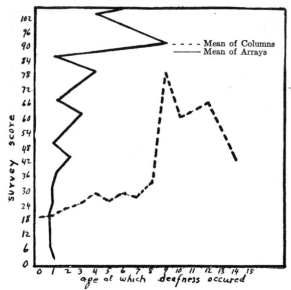

the fourth, fifth, sixth, and seventh years, although the curve is
uneven because of the small number of cases included at each
of these years. The Day Schools reveal the same general tendencies, except that the curve is less smooth. Instead of a plateau
in educational achievement from the fourth year to the seventh
there is a steady decline, but at the eighth year there is a large
increase, as was found in the Institutions.

Figures XXII and XXIII show the regression trends for the
relationship between chronological age and educational achievement, in the Day Schools and the 1,159 cases from the Institutions. The unbroken line, showing the prediction of chronological
age from Educational Survey Test score, is very interesting.
The general trend of the curve is the same for both types of
schools. There is a linear relationship between the two until a
score of about 50 is gained on the Educational Survey Test.
Scores about this point are not accompanied by increased chronological age. On the contrary, there is a slight tendency for these
high scores to be secured by younger children. This is especially
true in the Day Schools. A plausible explanation of this phenomenon is that the children who receive high educational scores

FIGURE XXII. DAY SCHOOLS. REGRESSION TRENDS FOR SURVEY TEST AND CHRONOLOGICAL AGE

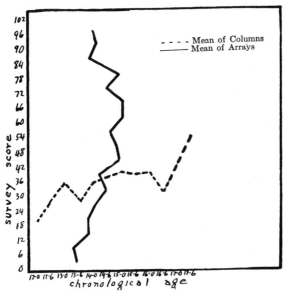

FIGURE XXIII. INSTITUTIONS (1,159). REGRESSION TRENDS FOR SURVEY TEST AND CHRONOLOGICAL AGE

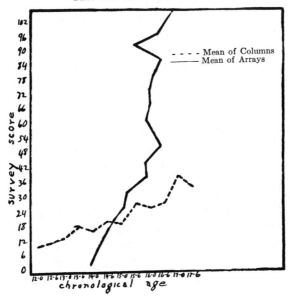

FIGURE XXIV.   DAY SCHOOLS.   REGRESSION TRENDS FOR SURVEY TEST AND
DEGREE OF RESIDUAL HEARING

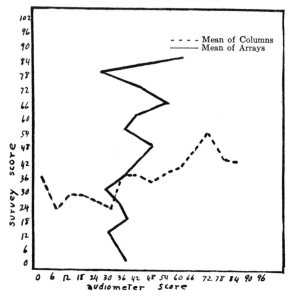

have become deaf relatively late in life, have attended a school for hearing children, and, as a result, achieve high educational scores at an earlier age than children who have been deaf all their lives and have not been able to profit by the teaching in a school for hearing pupils.

The broken lines for prediction of score on Educational Survey Test from chronological age are somewhat dissimilar in the two types of schools. In Figure XXII, showing the regression trend for the Day Schools, each six months' increase in age is accompanied by a relatively great increase in score on Educational Survey Test. After thirteen years of age, increase in chronological age is accompanied by practically no increase in educational achievement until the seventeenth year, when a definite advance is made. This is continued at age seventeen years six months. In the Institutions the gain in score on Educational Survey Test is relatively slight for each six months' increase in age until about the fifteenth year. Thereafter there is a slight tendency for increased educational gains to accompany successive increases in age.

FIGURE XXV. INSTITUTIONS (1,159). REGRESSION TRENDS FOR SURVEY
TEST AND DEGREE OF RESIDUAL HEARING

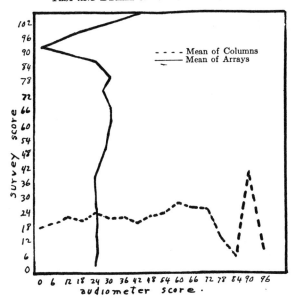

- - - - Mean of Columns
——— Mean of Arrays

Figures XXIV and XXV show the regression trends for the
relationship between score on Educational Survey Test and degree of residual hearing for the Day School group and for the
Institutional group of 1,159 cases. In the Institutions (Figure
XXV) the trend for predicting score on Educational Survey
Test from audiometer score rises slightly at first, then remains
practically level until 54 per cent of residual hearing is attained.
There is a fairly rapid rise in score on Educational Survey Test
for each unit of increase in residual hearing until from 60 per
cent to 65 per cent is reached. Pupils in the Institutions who
have a greater degree of hearing achieve, in general, a lower
educational score. This is probably due to the lower mental
ability of those in the Institutions who have a relatively great
amount of residual hearing. Apparently, very little use is made
of the residual hearing of the children by the Institutions, so
far as may be measured by the Pintner Educational Survey Test.

This is not true in the Day Schools (see Figure XXIV). Until
about 36 per cent of residual hearing is attained, increases in
audiometer score are not accompanied by increases in score on

FIGURE XXVI. DAY SCHOOLS. REGRESSION TRENDS FOR SURVEY TEST AND YEARS IN A SCHOOL FOR HEARING CHILDREN

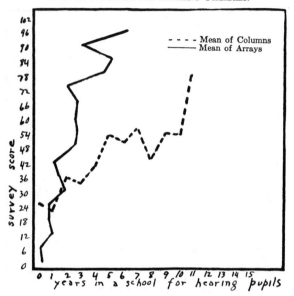

FIGURE XXVII. INSTITUTIONS (1,159). REGRESSION TRENDS FOR SURVEY TEST AND YEARS IN A SCHOOL FOR HEARING CHILDREN

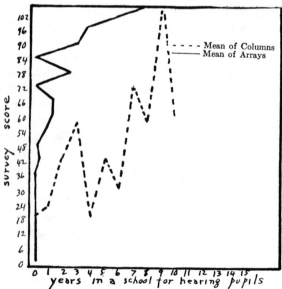

Educational Survey Test. At 36 per cent of residual hearing a sharp rise in educational achievement is made. This higher level of educational achievement is maintained by those with 36 per cent to 54 per cent of residual hearing. For every unit of increase in residual hearing from 54 per cent to 80 per cent, a marked increase in educational achievement is noticed. Apparently the Day Schools are making good use of the hearing which children possess. In the Day Schools, there are a number of children who possess degrees of residual hearing ranging from 54 per cent to 80 per cent. In the Institutions the proportion is smaller.

Figures XXVI and XXVII show the regression trends for the relationship between score on Educational Survey Test and years spent in a school for hearing children. In the Institutional group of 1,159 cases, the curve for predicting score on Educational Survey Test from years in a hearing school, is based on very small numbers, except for the part based on 0 to 0.9 years. The curve is consequently far from smooth. In the Day Schools (Figure XXVI) the cases are more numerous. The rapid rise in score on Educational Survey Test for each year spent in a school for hearing pupils is marked in both figures. In the Day Schools, relatively little improvement in the score accompanies increase in the years spent in a school for hearing children beyond five.

This study of Figures XIV to XXVII, showing the regression trends for each of the variables and Educational Survey Test score, emphasizes many of the points made in earlier chapters, in addition to showing more clearly the differences between the Day Schools and the Institutions. It also clearly shows the effect of given increases in each of the variables on educational achievement.

CHAPTER X

THE EFFECTS OF A FOREIGN LANGUAGE SPOKEN BY THE PARENTS

As in schools for normal hearing children in the United States many of the children in the schools and institutions for the deaf are of foreign birth or parentage. The questionnaire which was filled out for each child requested information about the language which is used most of the time in the home of the deaf child. Table 32 lists the various languages which were reported for both the Day School group and the Institutional group, with the frequency of occurrence. The table indicates only those cases in which the language most frequently used was foreign.

Table 33 shows how the 311 cases in Day Schools and the 1,470 cases in Institutions are distributed according to the reports made on the questionnaire.

A greater percentage of the children in the Institutions come from homes where English is the language most frequently spoken. The percentage of pupils in the Day Schools who come from homes where a foreign language is most frequently spoken is greater in the Institutions. It is interesting to note that 13.5 per cent of the replies from the Day Schools indicate that both English and a foreign language are spoken at home, and only 3 per cent of the replies from the Institutions make such a report. This is a difference of 10.5 per cent. If we consider as foreign all those who report that a foreign language is spoken at home, then we find that 39 per cent of the foreign parents in the Day School group speak both English and their native language, while in the Institutions only 25 per cent do this. This difference is 14 per cent.

The parents of the Day School pupils would appear to be becoming more Americanized than the parents of pupils in the Institutions. One explanation is found in the more urban character of the Day Schools, and consequently of the homes from

80

TABLE 32

LANGUAGE SPOKEN AT HOME IN THE DAY SCHOOL GROUP AND
IN THE INSTITUTIONAL GROUP

Day Schools				Institutions			
Language	Fre-quency	Per Cent of Total	Per Cent of Total Day School Group	Language	Fre-quency	Per Cent of Total	Per Cent of Total Institutional Group
Italian	26	39	8	Italian	40	28	3
Yiddish	20	30	6	Yiddish	32	22	2
Jewish	4	6	1	Polish	23	16	1.5
Polish	4	6	1	German	20	14	1.3
German	4	6	1	Russian	7	5	
Russian	2	3		Bohemian	6	4	
Slovanian	2	3		Lithuanian	3	2	
Armenian	1	1.5		Austrian	3	2	
Greek	1	1.5		Spanish	2	1.4	
Hungarian	1	1.5		Swedish	2	1.4	
Spanish	1	1.5		Flemish	1	.7	
				French	1	.7	
Total	66	99		Hungarian	1	.7	
				Jewish	1	.7	
				Slovanian	1	.7	
				Turkish	1	.7	
				Total	144	100	

TABLE 33

DISTRIBUTION OF QUESTIONNAIRE RESULTS INDICATING THE LANGUAGE
MOST FREQUENTLY SPOKEN AT HOME

Day Schools			Institutions		
Language	Frequency	Per Cent of Total	Language	Frequency	Per Cent of Total
English	198	64	English	1,203	82
Foreign	66	21	Foreign	144	10
Omitted	5	1.8	Omitted	76	5
Mixed	42	13.5	Mixed	47	3
Total	311	100.0	Total	1,470	100

which the children come. English is more necessary as a daily tool and is spoken part of the time at home.

The questionnaire returns showed 47 cases where the language spoken at home was not indicated, or where both English and a foreign language were spoken about equally. In this study of the comparison between the group whose home language is foreign and the English group reporting no foreign language in the home, these 47 cases are omitted.

It will be readily seen from Table 32 that in both the Day Schools and the Institutions the Italians are the most frequently represented, both in absolute number and in percentage of the foreign group. The percentage is not so high in the Institutional group as in the Day School group.

The group in which Yiddish is spoken at home holds second place in both types of schools. In the Day Schools these two groups account for 69 per cent of all the foreign element, whereas in the Institutions they account for but 50 per cent. The data available do not permit a statement of the reasons for this difference. It may be suggested however, that part of the explanation lies in the fact that the Day Schools draw from a more urban population coming from a more eastern portion of the United States than do the Institutions.

The number of different nationalities represented in the Day Schools is 11; the number in the Institutions is 16. In the Day School group 21 per cent of the total group studied are foreign, whereas only 10 per cent in the Institutions are in the foreign group. That is, only half as great a proportion in the Institutions speak a foreign language at home as is found in the Day Schools.

Early in this study it was stated that those cases for which the data were incomplete or inconsistent were discarded from consideration. In view of the relatively large group of pupils whose parental language is foreign the question arises whether the data for this foreign group showed a greater loss through incompleteness or inconsistency than the data for the group whose parental tongue was English. Table 34 gives the pertinent facts in relation to this problem.

The foreign group loses no greater percentage of the total number through incomplete or inconsistent data than does the group speaking English at home. So far as the questionnaire is concerned, the various Day Schools have been able to gather all the necessary facts as frequently from those whose home language is foreign as from those whose home language is English.

TABLE 34

COMPARISON OF ENGLISH AND FOREIGN IN REGARD TO COMPLETENESS OF DATA REPORTED ON THE QUESTIONNAIRE

Total number of foreign with incomplete data	81
Total number of English with incomplete data	235
Per cent that foreign are of total number with incomplete data	26
Per cent that English are of total number with incomplete data	74
Per cent that foreign are of total number with complete data	25
Per cent that English are of total number with complete data	75
Per cent that the foreign with incomplete data are of all the foreign	55
Per cent that the English with incomplete data are of the total number of English	54

The next question to be considered is: How does this group, whose home language is not English, compare with the group whose home language is English, in the various traits for which measurements are available?

In the Day School group, 198 cases were found whose parents speak English at home. The pupils of this group did not mention the presence of any other language as a means of communication in the home. Table 35 gives the means and sigmas for the group of 66 pupils who are foreign or of foreign extraction and the group of 198 pupils whose parents speak English at home.

Table 36 gives for each of the variables the difference between the means of the foreign and English groups with the standard error of this difference, the ratio of this difference to its standard error, and the chances out of 100 that the obtained difference is above zero.

The difference between the two groups in scores on the P.N.L. Test is such that there is no doubt that the trait measured by this test is found, on the average, to a lesser degree among the foreign group than among the English group. This is the only trait in which the difference is statistically reliable; that is, where the difference is more than three times its standard error.

However, the chances are more than 99 in 100 that the difference between the two groups in scores on the Educational Survey Test, and in the number of years spent in a school for the deaf is a difference which cannot be accounted for by chance. There are 49 chances to 1 that children of the foreign group start to school later than children of the English group, and

TABLE 35

COMPARISON OF THE MEANS AND SIGMAS OF THE FOREIGN AND ENGLISH GROUPS IN THE DAY SCHOOLS

Variable	Mean		Sigma	
	Foreign	English	Foreign	English
C. A.	14 yrs. 3.5 mos.	14 yrs. 8.8 mos.	18.29	19.76
P. N. L. Score	305.5	357.42	96.50	99.07
Survey Test Score	30.3	38.60	20.30	22.86
Audiometer Maximum ...	40.3	37.62	23.45	21.43
Years in Schools for Deaf .	5.76	6.73	2.62	3.10
Years in Schools for Hearing	1.92	1.95	2.20	2.59
Age of Starting to School .	7.70	7.05	2.26	1.61
Age of Becoming Deaf ...	3.06	2.45	2.67	2.89

TABLE 36

SIGNIFICANCE OF THE OBTAINED DIFFERENCE BETWEEN THE FOREIGN AND ENGLISH GROUPS IN THE DAY SCHOOLS

Variable	Difference Between Foreign and English in Day Schools*	S. D. of Difference	Diff. / S. D.$_{Diff.}$	Chances in 100 That Difference Is Significant
C. A.	+ 5.3	2.65	2.00	98
P. N. L. Score	+ 52.92	13.81	3.83	100
Survey Test Score	+ 8.30	2.98	2.79	99.74
Audiometer Maximum	− 2.68	3.27	.82	79
Years in Schools for Deaf ...	+ .97	.39	2.49	99.4
Years in Schools for Hearing	+ .03	.32	.09	.54
Age of Starting to School ..	− .65	.30	2.17	98.6
Age of Becoming Deaf	− .61	.39	1.56	94.

* + indicates that English group mean is higher; − indicates that foreign group mean is higher.

the chances are the same that the foreign children are younger than the English children.

The average age of becoming deaf for the foreign group is a little greater than for the English group. The chances are approximately 16 to 1 that this difference is not due to chance. The differences in degree of hearing and in the number of years spent in a school for hearing pupils can readily be accounted for by chance.

The more significant differences between these two groups are found in mental ability as measured by the P.N.L. Test, and in educational achievement as measured by the Pintner Educational Survey Test. But some of both these differences must be accounted for by the fact that the English group has almost certainly been in school longer than the foreign group. (The chances are 99 to 1.) The actual difference obtained comes to almost a year. To what extent the difference in mental ability and in educational achievement would be lessened if children who had been in school the same number of years were compared is not revealed.

In comparing the group of pupils in the Institutions who were reported as having a foreign language spoken most of the time at home, with the group which had English spoken at home, it was considered satisfactory to use the mean of the total Institutional group instead of tabulating and computing the English group separately. The amount of error involved will be small since only 10 per cent of the total group are foreign, and the differences in the variables are relatively small. The significant tendencies will be the same.

A comparison of the differences in Table 36 and Table 37 shows that the foreign group in both types of schools deviates in the same direction for chronological age, P.N.L. Test scores, Educational Survey Test score, audiometer maximum, and number of years in a school for the hearing. In the Institutional group, however, the foreign children have been in school a longer period. (The chances are 98.6 to 1.4 that the differences are due to other factors than chance.) And they have started to school younger. (This difference is statistically significant.) As was noted before, the foreign children in the Day Schools started to school later in life and have been in school a shorter period than the English group.

TABLE 37

SIGNIFICANCE OF THE OBTAINED DIFFERENCES BETWEEN THE FOREIGN
GROUP AND THE TOTAL GROUP IN INSTITUTIONS

Variable	Difference Between Foreign and Total Institutional Group*	S. D. of Difference	$\dfrac{\text{Diff.}}{\text{S. D.}_{\text{Diff.}}}$	Chances in 100 That the Difference Is Significant
C. A.	+ 4.80	1.75	2.74	99.7
P. N. L. Score	+ 11.45	10.43	1.10	86.
Survey Test Score	+ 3.14	1.42	2.21	98.6
Audiometer Maximum	− 3.62	1.62	2.23	98.6
Years in Schools for Deaf ...	− .48	.22	2.18	98.6
Years in Schools for Hearing	+ .08	.045	1.78	96
Age of Starting to School ...	+ .68	.18	3.78	100
Age of Becoming Deaf	+ .03	.13	.23	58

* + indicates that the mean for the total Institutional group is the higher; − indicates
that the mean for the foreign group is higher.

It is interesting to note the reversal in the rank order of the
ratios of the difference to the sigma of the difference in the Day
Schools and in the Institutions. In the former there is a greater
number of chances that there is a true difference between the
groups in mental ability than that there is a true difference in
educational achievement, while in the latter the reverse is true.
The chances are 1 to 6 that the obtained difference in the
P.N.L. Test scores would be zero, or in favor of the foreign
group, whereas there are 98 chances out of 100 that the difference
in Educational Survey Test score is significant. However, the
fact that in both types of schools, the differences are in favor
of the English group is additional evidence that the obtained
differences are indicative of the real facts.

Here again the data are not sufficient to make the dogmatic
statement that the foreign pupils do more poorly in their studies
than English children, for, although they have been in school a
greater number of years, they are not quite so old. Just what
effect this combination of factors makes on the results of the
P.N.L. Test and Educational Survey Test is not known.

Table 38 gives the same data as the last two tables, for the
foreign pupils in the Day Schools and the foreign pupils in the

Institutions. Chronological age, score on P.N.L. Test, and age of starting to school are not significantly different in the two groups. The chances are about 4 to 1 in each case that the difference is not caused by chance factors.

· TABLE 38

SIGNIFICANCE OF THE OBTAINED DIFFERENCES BETWEEN THE FOREIGN GROUP IN THE DAY SCHOOLS AND THE FOREIGN GROUP IN THE INSTITUTIONS

Variable	Difference*	S. D. of Difference	$\dfrac{\text{Diff.}}{\text{S. D.}_{\text{Diff.}}}$	Chances in 100 That the Difference Is Significant
C. A.	− .27	2.80	.96	83
P. N. L. Score	+ 12.80	15.50	.82	79
Survey Test Score	+ 10.10	2.84	3.52	100
Audiometer Maximum	+ 8.30	3.28	2.53	99.5
Years in Schools for Deaf ...	− 1.94	.37	5.24	100
Years in Schools for Hearing	+ 1.36	.27	5.04	100
Age of Starting to School ...	+ .28	.33	.85	80
Age of Becoming Deaf	+ 1.61	.35	4.60	100

* + indicates that the mean for the Day School group is the higher; − indicates that the mean for the Institutional group is higher.

The differences between the two groups in the other five variables are reliable.

Table 39 gives the ratio of the difference to the sigma of the difference for the total group from the Day Schools and Institutions, and also for the foreign group from the Day Schools and Institutions.

If it be assumed that the dichotomous trait, as well as the other trait, is normally distributed, the bi-serial r technique may be used to obtain another measure of relationship between the foreign group and the English group. This has been done for the Day School pupils for the scores on the P.N.L. Test and the Educational Survey Test. The resulting bi-serial r is .41. The standard error is .07. That for the survey is .29. The standard error is .08. In both cases there is a positive but not high correlation. There is a tendency for foreign pupils to receive mental and educational scores which are lower than those received by English pupils. The correlation, however, is not sufficiently high

TABLE 39

Ratio of Difference to the S. D. of Difference for (1) Total Day School Group and Total Group in Institutions and for (2) Day School Group and Institutional Foreign Group

Variable	Total Group	Foreign Group
C. A.	3.75	.96
P. N. L. Score	5.71	.82
Survey Test Score	9.07	3.52
Audiometer Maximum	7.30	2.53
Years in Schools for Deaf	5.17	5.24
Years in Schools for Hearing	9.46	5.04
Age of Starting to School	8.27	.85
Age of Becoming Deaf	7.12	4.60

to predict, in any given instance, that a foreign pupil will receive a score which will be below the score received by an English pupil.

The correlation in the case of the Educational Survey Test is lower than that with the P.N.L. Test. This is as one would expect from the results shown by the "significance of difference" technique. (The ratio of the difference to the sigma of the difference for the P.N.L. Test was higher than that for the Educational Survey Test.)

In the following bi-serial r's for the Institutions only every tenth case which was English was used. The total number of English cases used was 130. The number of foreign cases was 144. The means of this sampling were lower than the means of the whole group, being 22.5 for the Educational Survey Test instead of 23.3, and 303.5 for the P.N.L. Test instead of 304.1. Presumably both would be raised a little if only the English group were considered by itself, but the foreign group consisted of only 10 per cent and the differences are very small between the foreign group and the total group; it was not considered necessary, therefore, to isolate this large group. The bi-serial r would be raised a little if the means for the whole English group had been used instead of the sampling of 130. The sigma of the 274 cases in this sampling for the Educational Survey Test is 17.5. That for the whole group of Institutions is 17.5. The sigma for the P.N.L. Test for the sampling is 128.4. That for the whole group is 119.0. This difference would have a tendency to raise the obtained bi-serial r.

The bi-serial r between foreign-ness and scores obtained on the Pintner Educational Survey Test is .08. The S.D $_{r \text{ (bis)}}$ is .08. The bi-serial r between foreign-ness and scores obtained on the Pintner Educational Survey Test is .06. The S.D. $_{r \text{ (bis)}}$ is .08.

In the case of the Educational Survey Test the S. D. for the entire distribution is appreciably low because of the large number of undistributed zero scores. The test was very much too difficult for a considerable number of pupils in the Institutions.

The increase in the sigma would exert a negative influence on the correlation. However, the difference in the means is so small and the correlations obtained are so low that, so far as the large group studied is concerned, there is very little disadvantage to the child, either in mental ability or in educational progress, in coming from a home in which a foreign language is spoken most of the time.

This statement cannot be made about the group of foreign students found in the Day Schools. Here, there is considerable correlation between mental ability and foreignness, as measured in this study. The correlation is not high enough to enable one to predict the probable rating of an individual, but for a large group the relationship holds true. The bi-serial r of .22 between the Educational Survey Test scores and foreignness is positive but low. None of the correlations obtained enables one to predict that an individual child will receive a low score in either P. N. L. Test or Educational Survey Test because a foreign language is spoken in the home.

CHAPTER XI

OCCUPATIONS OF THE PARENTS

Information concerning the occupations of the fathers of the deaf children was obtained by means of the questionnaire. In some cases this item was not filled in. What influence these missing cases would have on the results hereafter reported, it is impossible to judge. It is possible, however, to find out if children of the foreign group contribute more than their share toward these unfilled blanks. Table 40 gives this information for the Day Schools and for the Institutions. It will be noted that in both Day Schools and Institutions a greater percentage of chil-

TABLE 40

PER CENT OF ENGLISH- AND FOREIGN-SPEAKING PARENTS
FOR WHOM NO OCCUPATION WAS REPORTED

Group	Per Cent of Parents for Whom No Occupation Was Reported	
	English-Speaking	Foreign-Speaking
Day Schools	12	7.5
Institutions	13.5	8

dren who speak English omit giving their fathers' occupations than those who speak a foreign language. Thus it is likely that the mean of the foreign group will deviate a little less widely than the mean of the English group when the occupations are rated on a scale. If, as frequently happens, the mean of those not replying is lower than the mean of those replying, the foreign group will be given more nearly their true rating than the English-speaking group.

In this study two scales for rating occupations are used. The first is that employed by the Institute of Educational Research of Teachers College, Columbia University,* in an extensive vocational study the results of which are to be published soon. This scale (referred to as I.E.R. Scale) rates the occupations on a 1 to 5 basis, giving a value of 1 to such non-skilled occupations as laboring, truck driving, and the like, and a value of 5 to professional occupations requiring college graduation.

Table 42 shows the great similarity in the means and sigmas of the two matched groups. It is only when the percentages in each group are examined, that the differences between the groups become apparent. The Institutions, as a whole, have a greater percentage of people in classes 1 and 4 than the Day Schools.

TABLE 41

I. E. R. OCCUPATIONAL RATING OF FATHERS OF DEAF CHILDREN

Scale Rating	Institutions 1,470 Cases	Per Cent of Total	Day Schools	Per Cent of Total	Diff.
5	32	3	9	3	0
4	441	37	66	24	+ 13
3	252	21	109	39	− 18
2	113	9.5	37	13	− 3.5
1	352	29.5	57	21	+ 8.5
Total	1,190	100	278	100	
Mean		2.76		2.74	
S. D.		1.28		1.30	

This is largely explained by the fact that among the Institutions "farmer" was given as the father's occupation in a great number of cases. According to the scale, a farmer who owned and operated his land was rated 4. The questionnaire did not give sufficient information upon which to decide whether the father was a farm laborer or a farm owner. Consequently, all farmers were rated 4. Their number was so great that the percentage for that rating was unduly high. However, this is counterbalanced by a greater percentage of 1 ratings, and a lesser percentage of 3 ratings than among the fathers in the Day Schools. The group of 311 from the Institutions has a tendency to approach in the direction of the distribution of Day School percentages, although

* The author is indebted to Mrs. Zaida Miner, Statistician to the Institute of Educational Research, for permission to use this scale.

TABLE 42

I. E. R. OCCUPATIONAL RATING OF FATHERS OF THE 622 MATCHED CASES

Scale Rating	Institutions 311 Cases	Per Cent of Total	Day School 311 Cases	Per Cent of Total	Diff.
5	7	2.5	9	3	− 5
4	97	36	66	24	+ 12
3	62	23	109	39	− 16
2	33	12	37	13	− 1
1	71	26	57	21	+ 5
Total	270	99.5	278	100	
Mean...........		2.76		2.74	
S. D.		1.25		1.30	

it is nearer in numerical quantity to the whole Institutional group than to the Day School group.

It is probable that the Day School distribution corresponds more nearly to that which would be obtained in an urban, and therefore more competitive, community than that of the Institution. Use was made of the contingency method of correlation to find the relation between occupational rating and (1) P. N. L. Test rating and (2) Educational Survey Test score. Since achievement on both tests is greatly affected by age, while father's occupation presumably is not, the factor of age was eliminated by using three age groups—thirteen, fourteen, and fifteen years. Table 43 gives the contingency coefficients obtained. For each of the Survey and occupation coefficients a 10 × 5 fold table was used. [39] This was also used in the thirteen-year-old group for the P. N. L. Test score and occupation because of one very low score. The two other coefficients are based on 8 × 5 fold tables.

When age is held constant there is a marked relationship between occupation and both mental ability and educational achievement. This is not nearly great enough to permit a prediction of a child's mental and educational rating, having given the child's age and the occupational rating of the father; but for groups, the coefficients are decidedly significant. The three coefficients for score on the Educational Survey Test are, on the whole, higher than for score on the P. N. L. Test. Apparently

TABLE 43

CONTINGENCY COEFFICIENTS BETWEEN THE I. E. R. OCCUPATIONAL RATINGS
AND SCORES ON PINTNER EDUCATIONAL SURVEY TEST AND
PINTNER NON-LANGUAGE TEST OF MENTAL ABILITY

Age Group	No. of Cases	Coefficient for Score on Educational Survey Test and Occupation	Coefficient for Score on P. N. L. Test and Occupation
13-year-olds	61	.61	.55
14-year-olds	52	.74	.54
15-year-olds	48	.66	.61

occupational status has a greater effect on school achievement than on mental ability as measured in this study.

The Barr Scale for rating occupational status was used as a check on the I.E.R. Scale. The scale as used is described in L. M. Terman's *Genetic Studies of Genius,* Volume I, pp. 67-68. This scale is much finer than the one which was used in the present study. The ratings run from 1 to 20. Accompanying each rating is a short description of the occupation. These descriptions were only occasionally helpful in the present study, for the reports on the questionnaire were very brief. Only in a few instances were descriptions given of the occupation. For example, "farmer" is rated on the Barr Scale at several different levels according to the size of the farm managed. The questionnaire revealed only whether or not farming was the father's occupation. If no description accompanied the word "farmer" the median rating for farmer was given.

The contingency method was again used to determine the relationship between the ratings of the occupations on the Barr Scale and the scores on the P.N.L. Test and the Educational Survey Test. Table 44 gives the coefficients.

Table 45 gives a comparison of the values of the contingency coefficients for the I. E. R. method of scaling and for the Barr method of scaling.

In plotting the values for the Barr ratings with each of the other two variables, the following kinds of tables were used. With the thirteen-year-old group and score on the P. N. L. Test a

TABLE 44

CONTINGENCY COEFFICIENTS BETWEEN THE BARR OCCUPATIONAL RATINGS
AND SCORES ON THE PINTNER EDUCATIONAL SURVEY TEST AND
PINTNER NON-LANGUAGE TEST OF MENTAL ABILITY

Age Group	No. of Cases	Coefficient for Score on Educational Survey Test and Occupation	Coefficient for Score on P. N. L. Test and Occupation
13-year-olds	61	.70	.65
14-year-olds	52	.78	.69
15-year-olds	48	.72	.68

TABLE 45

COMPARISON OF CONTINGENCY COEFFICIENTS OBTAINED
BY THE TWO RATING SCALES

Age Group	No. of	Coefficient for Score on Survey Test and Occupation		Coefficient for Score on P. N. L. Test and Occupation	
		I. E. R.	Barr	I. E. R.	Barr
13-year-olds ..	61	.61	.70	.55	.65
14-year-olds ..	52	.74	.78	.54	.69
15-year-olds ..	48	.66	.72	.61	.68

10×7 fold table was employed. In the other two cases an
8×7 fold table was used. In the thirteen-year-old group for the
Barr ratings with score on the Educational Survey Test, a
10×6 fold table was employed. In the other two tables 10×7
fold tables were used. A comparison of these tables with the
ones used for the I. E. R. ratings reveals the fact that the former
have a greater number of cells than the latter. This fact is a
partial, if not complete, explanation of the consistently greater
coefficients secured when the Barr scale is used.

Both rating scales reveal marked relationships between the
occupational status of the parent and (1) educational achievement, (2) the Pintner Non-Language Test score of the child
which is indicative of his mental ability. Both scales show a

higher relationship between occupational status and educational achievement than between occupational status and mental ability. This is as one would expect; for, in general, those higher in the occupational scale have had more schooling than those lower in the scale. Consequently, they are better able to instruct their deaf children. Since these coefficients are based upon Day School children, where the child spends part of his day at home, there is opportunity for this parental assistance.

It is interesting to note that the mean Barr rating for the English-speaking group of parents in the Day Schools is nearly the same as the one reported by Terman [34] for an unselected group of adults. The mean Barr rating for the English-speaking parents of the children in the Day Schools is **9.18.** That which Terman estimated for his unselected group of adults is **8.88** by method A, and **7.92** by method B. It would seem that, so far as occupational status is concerned, being the parent of a deaf child does not indicate that one is low in the occupational scale. The mean Barr rating for the foreign group is **7.81.** This is equivalent to such an occupation as butcher or baker. A rating of **9.18** is equivalent to such an occupation as bookbinder.

One other relationship between occupational rating and the other factors included in this study is interesting: that between occupational rating and speaking a foreign language in the home. The bi-serial r technique was used to discover this relationship. The coefficient is .25; S.D. (bis) is .085. This may be taken to indicate a low but significant positive relation between the two. However, the fact that a foreign language is spoken most of the time at home is not proof that a position with a high rating may not be held. Of the foreign group of **59, 41** per cent reach or exceed the mean of the group speaking English most of the time at home. The number in the English-speaking group is **173.**

A similar study of the Institutional group has not been attempted because of the very great percentage of "farmers" in comparison with the other occupations. The word without any description makes it impossible to give an accurate rating to this occupation. Hence, an analysis of relationships based on such data would be of little value.

CHAPTER XII

CONCLUSIONS

The following are conclusions derived from the analyses described in detail in the preceding chapters.

1. The difference between mental ability of Day School pupils and Institutional pupils is statistically reliable. The Day School selects the brighter children.

2. There is a statistically reliable difference between the Day School pupils and the Institutional pupils in educational achievement as measured by the Pintner Educational Survey Test.

3. Children who attend the Day Schools have, in general, a greater degree of residual hearing than children who attend the Institutions. Statistical certainty is attained.

4. Superiority in degree of residual hearing is accompanied by a later age of becoming deaf and a greater number of years spent in a school for normal hearing pupils. Statistical certainty is attained.

5. When the important factors of age and mental ability are made equal there is still a real difference in favor of the Day School pupils in educational achievement.

6. When, in addition to the factors just named, only those children in the Day Schools who have been deaf from the age of one year and who have never attended a school for normal hearing children are compared with similar children in the Institutions, the difference between the two types of schools is reduced slightly over fifty per cent.

7. The difference is still in favor of the Day Schools. With the 83 cases used there are 99 chances in 100 that the true difference would be above zero.

8. Since the process of equating, as indicated in conclusion 6, also equalized the factors of residual hearing, age of starting to school, and years spent in a deaf school, the conclusion must be reached that the chances are very great that the Day Schools

are superior to the Institutions in the type of education which is measured by the Pintner Educational Survey Test.

9. There are marked differences between the correlations obtained from the Day School group of 311 cases and the Institutional group of 311 cases. This is indicative of a divergence in the sampling of the two groups. This confirms from another point of view the conclusions just stated.

10. The correlations from the Institutional groups of 1,159 and 311 are markedly similar, indicating a similarity in the two samples. The slightly higher correlations for the group of 1,159 can be readily accounted for by the greater variability of this group.

11. The curvilinear relationship between Pintner Educational Survey Test score and Pintner Non-Language Test score is not usually found between educational achievement and mental ability among normal hearing children.

12. Unless there are selective factors operating, which are not revealed in this study, this curvilinear relationship may be interpreted as follows: Among deaf children it takes a relatively greater degree of mental ability to increase six units at the beginning of the educational scale than to increase six units from a score of 40. After a score of about 50 on the Educational Survey Test, there is little rise in Non-Language Test score to accompany a rise in educational score. Apparently children scoring about 400 and above on the Non-Language Test compete on about equal terms, so far as Educational Survey Test is concerned. This is true for both Day Schools and Institutions.

13. In both the Day School group and the Institutional group there is a marked curvilinear relationship between years spent in a deaf school and educational achievement. The relationship is more curvilinear in Day Schools than in Institutions.

14. The cause of this phenomenon seemed to lie in the fact that many of the children who have attended a school for the deaf a short period of time have attended a school for normal hearing children for part of their school lives. In these schools they acquired sufficient information to make a good score on the Educational Survey Test. Those who had spent less time in the hearing school and a little more in the deaf school, made a lower educational score. Then after a certain point, number of years in a deaf school is positively correlated with educational survey score.

15. The numerous curvilinear relationships among the variables prevent effective treatment by means of partial and multiple correlation.

16. There is a significant positive relationship between the presence of a foreign language spoken in the home and a low educational and mental score.

17. In general, among the foreign group those whose parents speak Italian at home are low in mental and educational ability, while those whose parents speak Yiddish are high.

18. Among the Day School children the percentage of those whose parents speak a foreign language at home is higher than it is among the Institutional children. This should constitute a handicap to the Day Schools in producing educational results.

19. The average occupational rating of the fathers of the Day School pupils and that of the fathers of the Institutional pupils are practically the same.

20. However, there are more of both very low and fairly high occupational ratings among the fathers of the Institutional children, while there are more average ratings among the fathers of the Day School pupils with fewer cases at the extremes.

21. So far as the influence of economic status as indicated by the occupation of the father on educational achievement and mentality is concerned, the two types of schools are evenly matched.

APPENDIX I

PROBABILITY TABLE FOR DIFFERENCES

The following table gives the chances in 1,000 that a true difference exists. It is based on the amount of the difference and the S.D. of the difference.

$\dfrac{\text{diff.}}{\text{S.D.}_{\text{diff.}}}$	Chances in 1,000	$\dfrac{\text{diff.}}{\text{S.D.}_{\text{diff.}}}$	Chances in 1,000
.00	500	1.25	894
.05	520	1.30	903
.10	540	1.35	911
.15	560	1.40	919
.20	580	1.45	926
.25	599	1.50	933
.30	618	1.55	939
.35	637	1.60	945
.40	656	1.65	951
.45	674	1.70	955
.50	692	1.75	960
.55	709	1.80	964
.60	726	1.85	968
.65	642	1.90	971
.70	758	1.95	974
.75	773	2.00	977
.80	788	2.10	982
.85	802	2.20	986
.90	816	2.30	989
.95	829	2.40	992
1.00	841	2.50	994
1.05	853	2.60	995
1.10	864	2.75	997
1.15	875	2.90	998
1.20	885	3.10	999

This table is read as follows:—If the difference between two measures is 3 and the standard deviation of this difference is 1.5 the ratio $\dfrac{\text{diff.}}{\text{S.D.}_{\text{diff.}}}$ will equal 2.00. Opposite 2.00 in the table is 977. There are 977 chances in 1,000 that the true difference (the difference between the true measures) is greater than zero.

APPENDIX II

The probable errors of the correlation coefficients and correlation ratios in this study may be readily determined from the following table [36]. Negative r's have the same probable errors as positive ones of the same absolute magnitude.

PROBABLE ERROR TABLE

Test Group	N	Range of r's and η's having P.E.'s of:				
		.04	.03	.02	.01	.00
Day Schools ...	311	.00–.29	.30–.58	.59–.77	.78–.93	.94–1.00
Matched Institutions ..	311	.00–.29	.30–.58	.59–.77	.78–.93	.94–1.00
Remaining Institutions ..	1159			.00–.47	.48–.86	.87–1.00

APPENDIX III

FORMULÆ USED IN THIS STUDY *

$$M = A + \left(\frac{\Sigma fd}{N}\right)I$$ [Mean for distribution]

$$\text{S.D.} = \sigma = \left(\sqrt{\frac{\Sigma fd^2}{N} - \left(\frac{\Sigma fd}{N}I\right)}\right)^2$$ $\left[\begin{array}{c}\text{Standard deviation}\\ \text{for distribution}\end{array}\right]$

$$\dagger \text{ S.D.}_M = \sigma_M = \frac{\text{S.D.}_{\text{dist.}}}{\sqrt{N}}$$ $\left[\begin{array}{c}\text{Standard deviation}\\ \text{for a mean}\end{array}\right]$

$$\ddagger \text{ S.D.}_{\text{diff.}} = \sigma_{\text{diff.}} = \sqrt{\text{S.D.}_{M_1}^2 + \text{S.D.}_{M_2}^2}$$ $\left[\begin{array}{c}\text{Standard error of}\\ \text{the difference be-}\\ \text{tween two uncorre-}\\ \text{lated means}\end{array}\right]$

$$V = \frac{100 \text{ S.D.}}{M}$$ [Coefficient of variation]

$$K = \sqrt{1 - r^2}$$ [Coefficient of alienation]

$$r = \frac{\dfrac{[\Sigma x^2 + \Sigma y^2 - \Sigma(x-y)^2]\,(N)}{2} - (\Sigma x)\,(\Sigma y)}{\sqrt{N[(\Sigma x^2) - (\Sigma x)^2]}\ \sqrt{N[(\Sigma y^2) - (\Sigma y)^2]}}$$ $\left[\begin{array}{c}\text{Toops [35] com-}\\ \text{putation form for}\\ \text{the correlation co-}\\ \text{efficient}\end{array}\right]$

* Symbols used in formulæ are those used by Holzinger [18] unless otherwise indicated.

† Huffaker and Douglass [19] make the following statement about the proper occasion on which to use $\dfrac{\sigma_{\text{dist.}}}{\sqrt{N}}$ as the standard error of a mean.

"If . . . one is making generalizations about some abilities or characteristics of all twelve year old boys, for example (an indefinite number of them) from obtained scores, one must use the formula $\sigma_{m_{e+5}} = \dfrac{\sigma_x}{\sqrt{N}}$."

This statement describes the purpose of computing the standard error of the means in this study.

‡ In finding the significance of the differences between the 311 matched pairs in Chapter V the short formula $\sigma_{\text{diff.}} = \sqrt{\sigma^2_{M1} + \sigma^2_{M2}}$ was used although the longer one was applicable. As Walker [37] has shown, the presence of positive correlation decreases the $\sigma_{\text{diff.}}$ and consequently increases the significance of the obtained difference. Since all the differences are very significant the labor of finding the necessary correlations was avoided by use of the short formula.

In finding the significance of the differences between the 83 matched pairs in Chapter VIII the longer formula $\sigma_{\text{diff.}} = \sqrt{\sigma^2_{M1} + \sigma^2_{M2} - 2\,r\sigma_{M1}\sigma_{M2}}$ was used.

In all other cases it seemed fair to assume that the correlation between the mean scores of pairs of samples would approach zero and that the short formula was applicable.

$$\text{P.E.}_{\cdot r} = \frac{\cdot 6745 \ (1 - r^2)}{\sqrt{N}}$$

$$\left[\begin{array}{c}\text{Probable error of corre-}\\\text{lation coefficient}\end{array}\right]$$

$$\eta_{yx} = \frac{\sqrt{\dfrac{\Sigma fx(M_y - \overline{Y}_x)^2}{N}}}{\sigma_y}$$

$$\left[\begin{array}{c}\text{Correlation ratio for}\\\text{means of columns}\end{array}\right]$$

$$\eta_{yx} = \frac{\sqrt{\dfrac{\Sigma fy(M_x - \overline{Y}_y)^2}{N}}}{\sigma_x}$$

$$\left[\begin{array}{c}\text{Correlation ratio for}\\\text{means of arrays}\end{array}\right]$$

$$\text{P.E.}\eta = \frac{\cdot 6745 \ (1 - \eta^2)}{\sqrt{N}}$$

$$\left[\begin{array}{c}\text{Probable error corre-}\\\text{lation ratio}\end{array}\right]$$

$$N(\eta^2 - r^2) < 11\cdot 37$$

$$\left[\begin{array}{c}\text{Blakeman's short test}\\\text{for linearity [17]}\end{array}\right]$$

$$r_{\text{bis}} = \frac{\overline{Y}_2 - \overline{Y}_1}{\sigma_y}\left(\frac{pq}{z}\right)$$

$$[\text{Bi-serial } r]$$

$$\text{S.D.}r_{\text{bis}} = \frac{\left(\dfrac{\sqrt{pq}}{z} - r^2\right)}{\sqrt{N}} \frac{\left(\dfrac{\sqrt{pq}}{z^2} - r^2\right)}{\sqrt{N}}$$

$$[\text{Standard error of bi-serial } r]$$

$$\text{C} = \sqrt{\frac{S - 1}{N}}$$

$$[\text{Computation form for contingency coefficient}]$$

$$r_{\text{oc}} = \frac{S}{\sigma_c} = \frac{\Sigma w_u r_{\text{ou}}}{\sqrt{\Sigma w_u A_u}}$$

$$\left[\begin{array}{c}\text{Salisbury [33] formula}\\\text{for computation of}\\\text{multiple correlation}\\\text{coefficient}\end{array}\right]$$

$$\text{S.D.}_{\text{diff.}} = \sqrt{\text{S.D.}^2_{\text{M1}} + \text{S.D.}^2_{\text{M2}} - 2\,r\,\text{S.D.}_{\text{M1}}\,\text{S.D.}_{\text{M2}}}$$

$$[\text{Standard error of difference between two correlated means}]$$

APPENDIX IV

REFERENCES

1. BEST, HARRY. *The Deaf*, Chap. IX. Thomas Y. Crowell, 1914.
2. BEST, HARRY. *The Deaf*, pp. 134-38. Thomas Y. Crowell, 1914.
3. BEST, HARRY. *The Deaf*, pp. 194-200. Thomas Y. Crowell, 1914.
4. BLAKEMAN, J. "On Tests for Linearity of Regression." *Biometrika*, 4, 1906, pp. 332-50.
5. DAY, HERBERT E., FUSFELD, IRVING S., AND PINTNER, R. *A Survey of American Schools for the Deaf, 1924-1925.* National Research Council, Washington, D. C., 1928.
6. *Deaf-Mutes in the United States, 1920.* Bureau of Census, Department of Commerce, Washington, D. C., 1923.
7. FLETCHER, HARVEY. "Some New Methods and Apparatus for Testing the Acuity of Hearing and Their Relation to Speech and Tuning Fork Methods." *Laryngoscope*, July, 1925, Vol. XXXV, No. 7, pp. 501-24.
8. I. S. F. "A Survey of Schools for the Deaf." *American Annals of the Deaf*, Sept. 1924, Vol. LXIX, pp. 313-19.
9. I. S. F. "The Survey of Schools for the Deaf, I." *American Annals of the Deaf*, 1925, Vol. LXX, pp. 391-421.
10. I. S. F. "The Survey of Schools for the Deaf, II." *American Annals of the Deaf*, 1926, Vol. LXXI, pp. 97-135.
11. I. S. F. "The Survey of Schools for the Deaf, III." *American Annals of the Deaf*, 1926, Vol. LXXI, pp. 284-348.
12. I. S. F. "The Survey of Schools for the Deaf, IV." *American Annals of the Deaf*, 1927, Vol. LXXII, pp. 2-34.
13. I. S. F. "The Survey of Schools for the Deaf, VI." *American Annals of the Deaf*, 1928, Vol. LXXIII, pp. 1-36.
14. I. S. F. "The Survey of Schools for the Deaf, VII." *American Annals of the Deaf*, 1928, Vol. LXXIII, pp. 184-201.
15. I. S. F. "The Survey of Schools for the Deaf, VIII." *American Annals of the Deaf*, 1928, Vol. LXXIII, pp. 273-98.
16. GARRETT, HENRY E. *Statistics in Psychology and Education*, p. 133. Longmans, Green, 1926.
17. GARRETT, HENRY E. *Statistics in Psychology and Education*, p. 210. Longmans, Green, 1926.
18. HOLZINGER, KARL J. *Statistical Methods for Students in Education*, pp. 360-65. Ginn, 1928.
19. HUFFAKER, C. L. AND DOUGLASS, KARL R. "On the Standard Errors of the Mean Due to Sampling and to Measurement." *Journal of Educational Psychology*, Dec. 1928, Vol. XIX, No. 9, p. 648.

20. KELLEY, T. L. "Principles Underlying the Classification of Men." *Journal of Applied Psychology*, 1919, Vol. III, No. 1, p. 50.
21. KELLEY, T. L. *Statistical Method.* Section 30, pp. 102-3 and 373-85. Macmillan, 1923.
22. PEET, ISAAC L. "History of the New York Institution for the Deaf and Dumb." *American Annals of the Deaf*, Vol. IX, 1857, pp. 168-84. Report of the New York Institution, 1843.
23. PINTNER, R. "The Survey of Schools for the Deaf, V." *American Annals of the Deaf*, 1927, Vol. LXXII, pp. 273-99.
24. PINTNER, R. "Group Tests After Several Years." *Journal of Educational Psychology*, Sept. 1925, Vol. XVI, No. 6, pp. 391-95.
25. PINTNER, R. "Results Obtained with the Non-Language Group Test." *Journal of Educational Psychology*, Nov. 1924, Vol. XV, No. 8, pp. 473-83.
26. PINTNER, R. "A Non-Language Group Intelligence Test." *Journal of Applied Psychology*, Sept. 1919, Vol. III, pp. 199-214.
27. PINTNER, R. AND FITZGERALD, F. "An Educational Survey Test." *Journal of Educational Psychology*, 1920, Vol. XI, No. 4, pp. 207-23.
28. PINTNER, R. AND MARSHALL, H. "A Combined Mental-Educational Survey." *Journal of Educational Psychology*, 1921, Vol. XII, No. 8, pp. 32-43 and pp. 88-91.
29. PINTNER, R. AND PATERSON, D. G. "A Measurement of Language Ability of Deaf Children." *Psychological Review*, Nov. 1916, Vol. XXIII, No. 6.
30. PINTNER, R. AND PATERSON, D. G. "Learning Tests with the Deaf." *Psychological Monographs*, 1916, Vol. XX, No. 4. Psychological Review Co., Princeton, N. J.
31. PINTNER, R. AND PATERSON, D. G. *A Scale of Performance Tests.* Appleton, 1917.
32. REAMER, J. C. "Mental and Educational Measurements of the Deaf." *Psychological Monographs*, No. 132. Psychological Review Co., Princeton, N. J., 1921.
33. SALISBURY, FRANK G. "A Simplified Method of Computing Multiple Correlation Constants." *Journal of Educational Psychology*, Jan. 1929, Vol. XX, No. 1, pp. 44-52.
34. TERMAN, L. M. *Genetic Studies of Genius.* Vol. I, pp. 67-68. Stanford University Press, 1925.
35. TOOPS, HERBERT A. "Solving Inter-Correlations by Polar Coördinates." *Journal of Experimental Psychology*, Feb. 1922, Vol. V, No. 1, pp. 68-75.
36. TOOPS, HERBERT A. AND MINER, ZAIDA F. "A Serviceable P. E. *r* Table." *Journal of Educational Research*, Jan. 1924, pp. 3-8.
37. WALKER, HELEN M. "Concerning the Standard Error of a Difference." *Journal of Educational Psychology*, Jan. 1929, Vol. XX, No. 1, pp. 53-60.
38. YERKES, ROBERT MEARNS (Ed.). *Psychological Examining in the United States Army.* Government Printing Office, Washington, D. C., 1921.
39. YULE, G. V. *An Introduction to the Theory of Statistics*, pp. 66. Charles Griffin & Co., Ltd., 1924.

DATE DUE